Dare to Believe

Dare to Believe

Formerly *Your Authority to Believe*

by

Herbert Mjorud

Creation House
Carol Stream, Illinois

First Printing—September, 1975
Second Printing—January, 1976
Third Printing—August, 1976

ISBN 0-88419-117-6

Library of Congress Catalog Card Number 75-22574

CONTENTS

INTRODUCTION

Time and again God has miraculously worked in my life. Before my conversion, I wondered if there really *was* a God. Even if He truly existed, I thought it ridiculous to believe that He worked supernaturally in the lives of people.

Early childhood experiences and my background at home set the stage for an exciting life adventure. This book is not so much an autobiography as it is a narrative illustrating the reality and power of God.

Most people spend an entire lifetime without faith. They have no awareness of God. They never even try to use supernatural gifts and powers within their grasp because they appear contrary to natural logic and instincts. Yet I have learned—with struggle and difficulty—that human beings have a right to supernatural gifts and powers. Through Jesus Christ we even have the *authority* to use them. This is an account of how I learned this truth.

Herbert Mjorud
Minneapolis, Minnesota

1

A SHEER WALL OF WATER

I was a practicing attorney in Seattle when Japan attacked Pearl Harbor. My law partner's Naval Reserve unit was activated, and he left for overseas duty. Able-bodied men not eligible for the draft were urged to get into a "defense industry." So as a father of two, I put aside my law practice and resumed commercial fishing, a trade I had learned from my father, a Norwegian commercial fisherman in Alaskan waters.

In the fall of 1944, when the tuna season ended, we began a new kind of fishing—catching soup-fin sharks with nets. The liver of this particular shark had the highest concentration of vitamin A known in any natural food, with about three hundred and fifty thousand units of vitamin A per gram, compared to cod liver with only about fifteen thousand units of vitamin A per gram. This made the price of the shark liver go from four dollars to twelve dollars per pound. Each soup-fin shark had about seven pounds of liver, so each shark was worth more than one hundred dollars. The soup-fin shark was the talk of fishermen along the entire Pacific rim.

Boats were converted for this type of fishing. The "Ellie IV," my boat, was among them.

The "Ellie IV" was a fifty-foot salmon troller. It was diesel powered and had the latest electronic gear. We rigged seven thousand two hundred feet of cotton gill net, cut it into individual nets six hundred feet long and eight feet wide, made so they could be tied together. When the nets were lowered into the water, a line was weighted with lead that took the net to the bottom. Then a cork line lifted the net eight feet off of the ocean floor. Hopefully, any soup-fin shark in the vicinity of the net became caught in the net. The sharks would "gill" in ten-inch mesh and tangle themselves into the net. All the fishermen had to do was pull them aboard. This proved to be lucrative fishing for many boats. However, it was a brand new kind of fishing. Little was known of the habits of the soup-fin shark. Fishing was hit and miss, but some boats did exceedingly well.

In November of that year, my three crewmen and I set a "string" of nets, half our entire supply, in seventy fathoms of water about twenty miles off the coast of Washington. We anchored half a mile away from a bouy that marked the end of our nets.

"Let's let our nets 'soak' overnight. We can haul them in tomorrow morning to see what kind of fishing we'll all have on this bank," I said. Arne, a veteran crew member, nodded and we went to our bunks.

About four o'clock the next morning, I was awakened by a strong jerking at our anchor cable. The boat heaved in choppy waters. A rough easterly wind came up, and by five o'clock the jerking was severe. I got up from bed, started the engine and engaged the clutch. I headed the boat into the wind before the strain on the cable caused it to snap.

At daybreak, the wind suddenly switched and slammed at us with gale force.

"Wake up! We've got a gale outside," I shouted down the hatch.

But before we could get the power driven winch started so we could haul in the anchor, the waves were rolling hugh combers. They broke heavily over the deck of our boat.

"We've got twenty miles of rough water ahead before we hit Neah Bay," I said as the crew struggled to the deck. "We'll take the waves on the quarter bow, but it's still going to be rough. So hang on."

We moved at half cruising speed because of the mounting waves. A direct course to our harbor at Cape Flattery would have put us directly in the trough of those waves. By quartering the waves, the boat worked more easily through the waves. This also made allowance for wind and wave drift.

By now we were on our way, with waves twenty-five feet high breaking over our deck. I was at the helm in the pilot house. Every time a wave crashed on the deck, water flooded the pilot house deck and sluiced down into the galley.

I was pleased at how the "Ellie IV" was taking the rough weather. She was a well-constructed vessel with two-inch planking on oak ribs, and an inner lining of another two-inch planking. She was completely decked so hatches could be battened down tight. Except for water coming in through the pilot house and that seeping through the portholes, she had no leaks of any consequence. We had been through heavy weather with her before. But I had never been in a storm like this.

I disengaged the "iron mike" (automatic steering device). It did not react quickly enough when the boat twisted and lurched in the heavy seas. When I saw an unusually large wave, I'd swing the helm wheel quickly to head the boat more directly into that wave. Then I'd grab the throttle and slow the speed of the boat at the same time.

After an hour, Arne looked outside. "Looks like heavier weather ahead," he warned. But his words were nearly lost in the roar of the storm. Then I saw a huge wave coming upon us like a building six stories high.

"Hold on!" I shouted and spun the wheel to turn into the wave.

The wave broke hard over us and the "Ellie IV" wallowed in the trough unprepared for the next wave.

"Here comes another! It's even bigger," one of the men called out.

"Hang on!" was all I could say. It looked like a sheer wall of water coming at us.

The boat moved up with that wave, then rolled to its side. Our mast was *below horizontal.*

"We're capsizing!" someone shouted.

We were carried to the crest of the wave then dropped abruptly like a toy into the trough. It was at least a twenty-foot fall. We were still on our side when the cabin hit the water with a thunderous clap. I felt as though we were being smashed to bits.

This is it! I thought. Under that sixty-foot wave, completely buried in the sea, I could see nothing but eerie grey-green water out the cabin windows. I began to think how, if we somehow escaped drowning, we might ride out the storm clinging to debris. But we'd still have to fight off the sharks. Water gushed through cracks in the doors and windows like small fountains. Certain that we'd never come out of that experience alive, I realized that I was not afraid to die. I was a believer—and, come the worst, I was ready. I had a deep calm that came from the Lord. I had been through other harrowing crises when I didn't have that assurance. I liked the difference.

But the "Ellie IV" came up out of the depths of the sea like a submarine. Miraculously, some unseen Force pushed at the submerged cabin and mast. The ship righted herself as she came up! Somehow our heavy-duty Atlas diesel engine never missed a beat and chugged along as though nothing had happened!

We seemed none the worse for the experience, and I turned the wheel to quarter against the waves once again. There were more coming at us, but none like the last ones. I breathed a prayer of thanks to God. Once again, with the Lord's help and presence, my life had been spared.

Arne came to the pilot house.

"We've lost our lifeboat and all that was in it. Turn around and we'll pick it up," he yelled.

He was an old "salt" of the sea with many years of experience. I shook my head, amazed that he would think of such a thing right then. I was glad just to have come out of the experience alive with the boat still seaworthy.

"I don't think we'll ever see that lifeboat again," I said. "But we ought to turn with the wind to check our ship for damage. So I guess we can look for it."

The twelve-foot lifeboat had been lashed to the lee side of the cabin with thick copper cables. They all had snapped in the heavy sea. We turned, going with the waves and directly before the wind, in order to inspect our gear to see if we could still hold course for harbor.

Arne went out on deck. He returned shortly.

"The front stay on the port side of the mainmast has snapped, but everything else is shipshape," he repeated.

That stay was made of five-eighths-inch steel cable. Evidently, it had snapped when the mast slapped the water as we fell from the ridge of the wave. If both cables had snapped, we would have lost the mainmast as well as the foremast.

Arne had kept an eye out for our lifeboat. "Lifeboat off starboard bow!" he called shortly over the roar of the storm.

Sure enough! We all spotted it, bobbing in the angry sea, full of water. I eased the ship toward the lifeboat. The men, who were all on deck by now, grabbed hold of it. They waited for a high wave and pulled it aboard.

"Turn it over and empty the water," I ordered. "Then lash it behind the mainmast."

After rescuing our lifeboat, I turned the ship to a quartering tack again, heading into the big waves and slowing the motor. We were still in terrible weather with constantly roaring gale-force winds and breaking waves. But none was as bad as those two waves which had buried us in the sea. Six hours later we came into lee of land from Cape Flattery and calmer waters. With a tremendous sense of relief, I anchored the "Ellie IV" in the sheltered waters of Neah Bay.

The storm continued to rage for a week. We learned later that it was one of the worst storms ever to hit that part of the Pacific—with winds of more than one hundred miles per hour.

When it quit we went out to that same bank to pull our nets—if they were still there. They were! We found many soup-fin sharks entangled in them. Not only had God spared our lives and ship, He had given us a bonus. We grossed over four thousand dollars from our haul, a good share for each man on the good ship "Ellie IV."

During the six days we waited out the storm in the harbor, I had plenty of time to think. I thought about how close to death we had come. Our deliverance was a miracle indeed.

I had been converted to Christianity shortly before this incident, at the age of thirty-two. Looking back, I recalled many early steps of obedience along the way. Some did not seem important at the time, but in retrospect they determined my growth and development as a disciple and servant of Jesus Christ.

2

OTHER CLOSE CALLS

The Christian life is one of obedience training as well as learning. It's like breaking a colt. Training makes it an obedient animal, subject to its master. Likewise, Christ brings disciples into His will to make them obedient to His will.

There are trials involved in becoming subject to God. Yet, through disciplined obedience, we experience peace, joy, and abundant living.

Just as a colt is difficult to break and train, so are we. Our Master, however, is gentle and patient in His training. Progressive steps and nudges lead us into obedience that we might become something "to the praise of His glory."

Life is made up of a host of decisions and circumstances which call for reactions from us. These are woven into the fabric of life's training as we become conformed to the likeness of Jesus Christ.

Often we are not even consciously aware of the Lord's presence. But there are some circumstances through which He shows Himself and His concern for our lives. Some of these incidents can make deep impressions on us. They are like milestones along the way. Our miraculous escape from drowning was just one incident. There had been many others. I reflected over God's miracles in my earlier life.

I was born in 1910, delivered by a midwife on a Minnesota

farm. My parents were immigrants from Norway, having come to the United States the year before my birth.

At age twenty, Dad came to America. He had turned such a rebel at home that his family thought the trip might mellow him. Hearing about San Francisco and its gold, he went there to seek a fortune. However, things were not as he expected. Saturday nights were for saloons, dances and parties. Drinking early became a problem in his life.

Dad's adventurous spirit led him and other young men to board a steamer for Kodiak, Alaska. He found his place as a commercial fisherman, his strong body equal to the rugged work. While in Kodiak, he panned enough gold from a stream to make a wedding ring for Magna Melby, the young girl he left behind.

He returned to Norway, and they were married. But his spirit was restless. The thrill of his adventures in America called him back.

He was determined to become an Alaskan fisherman and contracted to have a thirty-six-foot salmon troller built. He cut labor costs by working on it evenings and Saturdays.

In March 1916, the troller, "Magna," named after my mother, was completed. Dad took his family aboard and headed for Alaska. We were four children by then: Hedy, myself, Sarah and Jane.

The first few days were beautiful as we chugged through the narrow protected channels. However, soon there were huge rolling waves, and it wasn't long before there were five very seasick passengers aboard the "Magna," crowded into the little fo'c'sle. Only Dad was unbothered by the rolling sea.

Eight days later, we came to Alaska's first port, Ketchikan. Dad decided for mother's sake that we should settle in Petersburg, a good place to rear children. Besides, ninety percent of the people were Norwegian and newly come to America.

When I was ten, Dad took me out during the summer on his fishing boat.

"I'm going to train you to become a deckhand. It won't be long before I'll have you cookin' and workin' like a seasoned sailor!" he said confidently.

I learned quickly and in many ways helped Dad as he fished for king salmon. Occasionally, he let me bring in a small salmon. At fourteen, I could land the largest of salmon, and when I was sixteen, I actually earned money teaching other men how to fish.

But each year Dad was given to more and more drinking. I knew that this had something to do with his cantankerous ways. He had rejected Jesus Christ in his youth and had become self-centered and almost psychotic, a very difficult person to live with. In his drunkenness, he often hit my mother or one of us for no apparent reason. Usually we were glad when he left on a trip.

My dad and mom were nominal Lutherans when they came to America. They had us children baptized in the Lutheran church, but church attendance was practically nil. Occationally as a boy, I went to Sunday School in the local Petersburg Lutheran Church. I still vividly recall the Bible stories and learning about the life of Christ. But by the time I was eight, I was through with Sunday School.

I respected my mother. She was the opposite of my father. He always put down me as well as everyone else in the family. But my mother loved and believed in me. She encouraged me in everything I undertook, especially in school.

"You have such a good mind," she'd say. "You are talented. All you have to do, Herb, is to apply yourself patiently, and you can excel in everything."

Because of her, I was able to ignore the negative taunts of my father.

My excuse for not taking confirmation instruction was that I was too busy. I had regular chores at home. Keeping the wood and coal boxes full, for both the kitchen range and living room heater, was my job. I felled trees or caught floating logs in the narrows of the nearby bay. With a drag saw, I sawed the logs into blocks, then used an axe to split the blocks. The chickens also were my responsibility, much to my chagrin. Feeding them and cleaning out the coops were really hated tasks.

I also had several ambitious projects to make money. I sold

newspapers, dug clams, and collected junk. When in season, I'd fish and hunt. I even picked berries. Besides all this, I still had time for sports, hiking, mountain climbing and rowboating.

But I never learned to swim well. The coastal waters were too cold for swimming, and as a result, I had two close calls of near drowning.

When I was ten, I was fishing off my dad's fishing boat, anchored in the harbor. Somehow, I leaned against a loose rope from the mast, lost my balance, and fell overboard. Sea water soon soaked my heavy mackinaw coat, and the weight pulled me under. I flailed and choked at the icy brine. Since I couldn't swim, the tide took me away from the ship.

My father was visiting another fishing boat, sitting in the fo'c'sle, drinking coffee. Suddenly, he had a premonition.

"Herb!" he shouted and ran to the deck.

Without knowing why, he jumped into his small skiff and rowed desperately toward his own ship. Just as I was going down for the last time, Dad spotted me. He lunged out quickly, grabbed me by the hair and pulled me aboard the skiff. He rowed quickly to our fishing boat and somehow carried me on deck. He gave me artificial respiration and revived me.

When we talked about it later, Dad could not explain his supernatural premonition which somehow stirred him to action.

Two years later, I was dipping for minnows with a bucket from a slip where fishing boats were moored. I slipped on the wet footing and plunged overboard again. This time I could dog paddle somewhat, but couldn't buck the current.

The tide swept me toward a dock. Desperately, I clawed at the piling and caught it. I swallowed water and choked as it spilled into my lungs. I tried to yell for help but no sound came out.

While clinging to that piling, I had a flashback of memory. My whole life unreeled before me in a matter of seconds. I recalled all the wrong things I had done. I knew I was not right with God. I believed I was headed for hell if I drowned. Then a fisherman sighted me losing my grip from the piling. He got to me in a rowboat just in time to save me from sure drowning.

Once more, death came inches close.

About one month before high school ended, I was on Chris Olson's boat to help rig gear. I recall smelling gas as I came aboard and remarked about it to Chris.

"Yes, that's because I filled some gas tanks yesterday," he said.

Since it was cold, Chris started to make a fire to warm up the fo'c'sle where we'd be working.

"Do you have a match?" Chris asked.

"No . . . wait a minute. Yes, I do have one."

I seldom carried matches but this time had one. I walked a few steps toward Chris and gave him the match. When he struck it, the boat exploded!

All I saw was a flash of light. The next instant the cabin was gone, and I saw the clear blue sky. The cabin blew several hundred feet into the air and crashed to bits on a nearby dock! Windows were blasted out of buildings on the dock.

We were both stunned but somehow conscious. We scrambled out of the boat to the mooring float. In minutes the boat sank. We watched sea water bubble in through the ribs which the blast had pulled loose from the keel.

Then my eyes widened in horror as I saw a huge hole where the storage battery was blown right through the side of our boat. If Chris had not asked me for a match, I would have been standing in the path of that battery and probably been crushed to death! But because I had a match and walked three steps toward Chris, I was beside him at the center of the explosion. Miraculously, both our lives were saved.

I thought about these incidents as the "Ellie IV" bobbed at anchor in Neah Bay. In the back of my mind I wondered why my life had been spared.

I didn't realize then that God was eager to demonstrate His presence to His children in visible, tangible ways. Since those days my adventures with Him have been even more exciting. I have been slow to learn. But it has been a rewarding experience to discover the secrets of God's miracle-working power and be able to exercise the authority we have as believers in Him.

In my own case, my selfish, stubborn ego often got in the way. In fact, I nearly blocked God from working at all in my life!

3

CREW CAPTAIN
AT THE UNIVERSITY

After graduation from high school, I bought my first fishing boat. I planned to fish all summer to finance college in the fall. But fishing was poor that year. In order to have enough money for college, I had to sell my boat. The proceeds paid my way to Seattle to enroll at the University of Washington as a pre-law student.

There were many adjustments for me to make, coming to the large city from a small town and to my new environment and surroundings. I was an honor student and basketball star in Petersburg. I had been at ease in the classrooms. But now I found myself timid and fearful in my new situations. The first time I was called upon for oral recitation in class, I got a mental block and couldn't say a word.

I found something, however, that did help my self-confidence. Since I had been named to the All-Alaska basketball team, I fully intended to play basketball at the University. I went down to the field house to look over their facilities. While there, another student came up to me.

"Hi, I'm Bill Stober."

"I'm Herb Mjorud from Alaska. Where do you come from?"

"I'm from Lewiston, Idaho," Bill replied. "Are you here to sign up for football?"

I shook my head. "Basketball is my sport."

"But that's not for several months. Why don't you join me in going out for football? You've got the build for a good football player."

I had no previous experience but Bill talked me into signing up for football practice to begin the following Monday.

Leaving the field house, Bill suggested, "Let's go down and see what's going on at the shell house."

"What's the shell house?" I asked, demonstrating my ignorance.

Bill patiently explained that the shell house was where the school stored racing shells for eight-oared rowing.

"That's where we six-footers come to try out for the rowing crews. Surely you've heard of the famous Washington rowing crews?"

I had to admit I had never heard of them, either. We came to the shell house where they were already in full swing of fall practice sessions.

"The frosh will be out in 'Old Nero,'" explained Bill. By now he knew I needed more background. " 'Old Nero' is a long flat barge, where freshmen learn the fundamentals of rowing."

When I got my first look at "Old Nero," I couldn't believe my eyes.

"It looks like an old galley slave ship out of the past!" I said in amazement.

It had eight oars on either side, one man to the oar. There were several men—called coxswain—in the rear. They were steering and shouting instructions through megaphones. The coaches also were shouting with megaphones. To me the din sounded like a flock of seagulls fighting for fish entrails, and I smiled at their ragged handling of the oars.

Having been reared on the water, boats and rowing were second nature to me. Bill turned to me.

"Want to try out?"

I nodded and followed Bill and the coach into the locker room. With the crew manager's help, we were soon outfitted with a sweatshirt, rowing pants, and rowing shoes.

"Well, let's go take on 'Old Nero,' " I said.

Bill and I were two of sixteen oarsmen in that lumbering old boat. I took a starboard seat and Bill a port seat opposite me. Each of us had a twelve-foot oar and sat on a rolling seat. Our feet were strapped in footboards so we could pull ourselves forward to a starting position once we had taken a stroke with that oar.

We manuevered the barge out into deeper water. When we came to the channel leading to Lake Washington, Coach Tom Bolles lectured us on some of the basics of rowing an eight-oared shell. Then he had us begin our first attempt at rowing the barge. We began by using just our arms and not the rolling seat.

It was easy, and I enjoyed the sport immediately—but I noticed nearly everyone else was having trouble. Many had absolutely no experience in handling an oar. Even Bill was having a hard time of it.

"Old Nero" was about eight feet wide with an aisle in the center for the coaches. As we paddled along, Coach Tom Bolles went from man to man, encouraging and giving instructions. When he came to me, I was surprised that he remembered my first name.

"Herb, you already have a sense of timing! You know how to handle an oar. With your strength, you'll have no difficulty in making the frosh crew. In fact, I'd say you've got the makings of a three-letter varsity crewman. Yes sir, that's my prediction for you!"

That did it for me. Every afternoon, except Sundays, Bill and I were at the shell house. We trained for six weeks, first in "Old Nero."

Then we "graduated" to a shell barge, sixty feet in length and twenty-six inches wide, round on the bottom. It was powered by eight oarsmen, with a coxswain to steer and shout orders from the coach. This shell barge was very difficult to ride on even keel. It lurched from side to side as we tried to row in unison. But after several months, we mastered the shell barge. We not only could ride it on even keel, but put power in each oar stroke.

Then it came time to try the racing shell itself.

These boats were sixty-two feet in length, only eighteen

inches wide, round like a log on the bottom. To do his coaching, Tom Bolles followed along in a motor launch, shouting instructions from a megaphone. He worked patiently with us day after day. After nine months of training and conditioning, we were ready for our races. We were scheduled to row against Oregon State frosh in May. Two weeks later, we faced our arch rivals, the California Bears. Our eyes were on the National Regatta on the Hudson River in New York, the first week of June.

Bill and I were both in the frosh crew of 1930. We won handily over Oregon State. We beat the California Bears by an unprecedented six lengths two weeks later.

In the National Regatta at Poughkeepsie, however, our number-six man collapsed from lung congestion a half mile from the finish line. He had to quit rowing, and the team could not keep up the rowing cadence. Our lead dwindled. Then a shell edged ahead of us. Then another just at the finish. We came in third, but still ahead of five other crews.

The prophetic words of frosh coach, Tom Bolles, came true, for I did row on the varsity crew for three years. The climax of my rowing days came in 1933, my senior year, when I was captain of the varsity rowing team. We won every race that year as well as the National Championship.

Following the championship honors, I was nominated by the Seattle *Post Intelligencer* for the Sullivan Trophy, given to the man or woman who had done the most to advance the cause of sportsmanship in the United States during the year.

Rowing was my life during those four years of college. The years went by swiftly. I worked in the field house laundry four hours, six days a week. I was paid $50 per month. I worked from seven to eleven in the morning, went to classes from eleven to four in the afternoon, and rushed down to the shell house immediately after my last class. Evenings were for study. There were no dates, no parties.

I gradually overcame my shyness. Sports gave me self-confidence. I also was voted into the Oval Club, an honor society. My last year I was elected to Fir Tree, one of twelve selected each year "for meritorious service to the University of Washington."

Yet, I had no knowledge of my destiny in the Kingdom of God during those years.

There was no contact with the church during my college days. I had one instructor, however, who shook our entire class one day. His parting words came on his last day as a professor at the University.

"I know this may come as a complete surprise to many of you. And I'm aware that what I say may infringe on school ethics, but I must say it anyway. There are many pursuits in life. Quite a few vocations are worthwhile in themselves. But unless these pursuits and vocations take *spiritual values* into consideration, they are all hollow and vain. Apart from Jesus Christ, all of life is a meaningless hodgepodge. I have found Christ as the answer to my life, and I am commending Him to all of you. That is my parting word to you. May God be in all of your lives."

Many of the students, including myself, were agnostics. We dismissed his testimony as archaic and irrelevant. But there was such a ring of sincerity and conviction in his voice that no one misunderstood what he was talking about.

We talked about the professor's "getting religion." One girl mocked his talk. Another student rebuked her.

"You really can't fault the old guy. At least he stood up for his convictions."

It was all very puzzling to me.

4

MY FIRST CALL TO GOD

I was an ardent agnostic. I often argued against and debated the existence of God.

"Religion is for the weak and old, women and children, but not for a virile and thinking man like myself. Besides, I've heard that the Bible is full of contradictions. We shouldn't waste our time reading it," I told anyone who'd listen.

But the words of Professor Wintermute struck deep. Mysteriously, they penetrated the darkness of my soul. A shaft of light began to stir up a restlessness. Then this unusual awareness left me. I was not to be troubled by it again for several years.

Each summer brought me back into commercial fishing on the high seas. Profits from this trade, together with my earnings from the laundry job at school, made me financially independent.

My graduation in the summer of 1933 concluded one chapter in my life and introduced another. I met and courted the woman who became my wife. Gundhild Anderson worked as a bookkeeper and clerk in a general store and fish-buying company in the village of Port Alexander, Alaska. Our friendship bloomed into romance.

Gundhild was a boon to my lonely soul. She had come here from her native Norway at age fifteen, one of eight children.

She had all the Norwegian graces of hospitality and homemaking. She was an excellent cook, could sew and knit beautifully, and do many other practical things. Our time together was spent on picnics, hiking, mountain climbing, and outdoor activities.

One evening we were out walking and stopped beside a small shaded grove. I could tell something was troubling Gundhild.

"What is it, darling?" I asked.

She didn't answer immediately, seemingly trying to frame her words. Finally she asked quietly, "Herb, do you believe in God?"

"Well, no. How could I? I don't know if there even *is* a God."

I was more curt than I needed to be and sensed I had hurt her. Her question seemed to express a hope that my answer would be affirmative. While not quite an atheist as some free thinkers at the University, I doubted the existence of God but was willing to concede belief if anyone could *prove* His existence.

I could see Gundhild's eyes glisten with tears.

"I'm sorry," I said, "but I have to be honest. I just have no logical reason to believe in God or turn to religion. But I'll have no quarrel if you do."

"When we are married and have children," she said, "they are going to be baptized and reared in the Lutheran Church."

Her response was an ultimatum spoken with such firmness that I knew no argument would change her mind. I decided to let the matter drop.

Gundhild was a believer since her conversion in childhood. We both sensed that the subject of God and religion was not going to be dealt with lightly. Yet neither of us wanted a conflict over the subject. We were both too much in love and didn't want to face the issue head-on since we were both afraid the other might walk away for good. I conceded to Gundhild on the practice of her own faith and instruction for our children when they would come along. And Gundhild did not try to discuss my agnostic beliefs or try to convert me.

After our marriage, she continued as a clerk-bookkeeper and I as a commercial fisherman in the summer months.

Meanwhile I enrolled at the University of Washington Law School.

I enjoyed the study of law, but it demanded a discipline and application that I had never known before. My lifestyle rebelled against the long hours of concentrated study.

I passed the first year with above-average grades, but many of my classmates flunked. The mortality rate was high in law school. Only thirty-three of the ninety-two who started made it to graduation.

In the spring of my second year, our son, Alton, was born.

Six weeks later, Gundhild and the baby were on their way to Port Alexander, Alaska, aboard a steamer. She was to resume her job and I was to follow after my final exams, about two weeks later.

When I did arrive, I had the task of tuning the engine of the "Chickadee," a thirty-foot salmon troller I had bought the summer before. I beached the "Chickadee" and painted the entire boat, then rigged her for the fishing season. Many boats had already tried various banks, but the fishing was poor. I had missed nothing thus far in the season.

But shortly after I arrived in Alaska, Alton became ill. Finally, a medical intern came to town. Hurriedly, we took the baby to him for diagnosis and treatment. He took one look and shook his head.

"Your baby needs immediate surgery. Unless he has this surgery, he will die," he said.

We wired our doctor in Seattle, giving him the diagnosis and symptoms. The next day, we had a return wire: "Feed baby cream of wheat porridge. If he does not respond in twenty-four hours, bring to Seattle." A local nurse volunteered to help during the five-hour trip. Gundhild's voice was weak as she boarded the plane, but she smiled courageously.

"Herb, it will all work out. Don't worry."

But I had lost all hope. Our boy was a pathetic bundle of skin and bones. He was so weak I doubted he'd even survive the trip to Seattle.

Gundhild had been praying and had hope in God. I returned to our apartment and threw myself on the bed. I sobbed as I had never done before. Grief and remorse weighed heavily on me. I wanted to pray but couldn't. Inwardly I cried, "Oh God, if there is a God, help us!"

The next morning I walked aimlessly. Then I boarded my fishing boat and thought. *I might as well pass the time fishing.* I started the engine, cast off the lines and headed for the fishing banks.

After running about an hour, my thoughts for Alton and Gundhild were diverted when I saw gulls and herring break the water. They were sure signs of fish. I lowered my fishing poles, slowed the boat to trolling speed and let out my gear. Right away I caught my first king salmon of the season, a twenty-pounder. I made short tacks back and forth. I caught another fish practically every time I passed the place where the gulls and herring were feeding. By late evening I had caught thirty-five king salmon, a good day's catch. They'd gross seventy or more dollars when I sold them that evening.

The Lord knew what to do for me. My son was "in the valley of the shadow," and I was desperately worried. My concern was eating away at me, so I needed this distraction. I had no time to think about my troubles after landing the first fish.

The following day I left harbor at daybreak with a fleet of boats. But the day was a waste. No one caught fish. Loneliness and sorrow set in quickly as I worried about my son. I even rehearsed plans for a funeral, thinking what I'd say to try to comfort Gundhild.

I left the banks late that afternoon. When I came ashore, I was handed a cablegram. My hands shook as I tore it open. *"Surgery successful. Alton took food one hour after surgery. Love Gundhild."*

Men on the dock smiled and encouraged me as I cried tears of joy. My son was alive!

Ten days after their arrival in Seattle, I received another cablegram. *"Will leave tomorrow on Steamer 'Alaska' with Alton in good health."*

"Thank God!" I cried. "Thank God, everything is all right." It was a miracle that Alton did not die on the long flight to Seattle. It was another miracle he could survive the operation.

Miracles? God? In the back of my mind a glimmer of belief flickered. Agnosticism wavered slightly.

But it wasn't too long before I was once again secure in my doubts and irreligious attitudes. Yet God was not content to let me be. I soon was to be shaken by a series of events more startling than any of the crises I faced as a boy or with our sick baby. There would be no escaping the supernatural power and presence of God!

5

"LEAVE ME ALONE"

My conversion to Christianity finally came after many "interferences" by outside, supernatural incidents. Each, by itself, did not cause me to think twice. Yet, over more than twenty years of such experiences, I began to sense the cumulative weight of them. I saw that there seemed to be a supernatural Force at work in my life. The incidents in my childhood were such that even a committed agnostic like me could not lightly dismiss them as coincidence.

The experience of seeing our baby restored from the verge of death was astonishing. By itself, the incident probably could be explained in purely natural terms. Yet, in the context of our lives, it moved me greatly. I could not explain it. At times I found myself even wanting to believe in God, in spite of my long years of unbelief. The Lord was showing His power and love in my life and I had to go out of my way to ignore Him. But I deliberately avoided the prompting of His Holy Spirit to believe.

Now things returned to normal. Alton recovered and began to grow. I fished that summer and worked all year to pay for the costs of chartering the plane, as well as the medical bills.

In 1938, I graduated with honor grades from law school. I had purchased a half-interest in a large troller, the "Ellie IV," with a cruising range that made it possible to fish anywhere

30

between California and Alaska. Fishing paid my way through law school and provided funds while I began the long, slow process of establishing myself as an attorney.

I looked for work in a law office. The best offer I received was seventy-five dollars per month. One of my classmates, Warren Ploeger, met with the same discouragement. One day he had an idea.

"Herb, what do we have to lose? Why don't we try and set up general practice as partners?"

This we did renting office space on the eleventh floor of Smith Tower in downtown Seattle.

The first months of any law practice bring in very little income. Our business was no exception. Any civil case booked for trial was at least two years away. Likewise, any fees for completed casework waited until that time. We knew this and did not allow lean financial returns for the first year to deter us. We agreed that I should spend the summers of the next few years fishing while we built our practice. Warren was not married and was living at home at that time, so he had no real financial problems.

This pattern became my lifestyle—fishing commercially in the summer so that I could afford to practice law the rest of the year.

It was many years after God's last "interference." I never gave Him a second thought until one day in 1941.

I was standing beside my secretary's desk, dictating a letter, when there was a rap at our door. Law offices always are open to the public, so a knock is rather unusual. I went to the door and was surprised to see my-youngest sister, Jane. She was married and the mother of two children. I knew she was having marriage trouble.

Jane wants a divorce and has come to me to represent her, the thought occurred to me. But I had no desire to enter into a family squabble as an attorney for one side.

My apprehension was quickly dispelled. Jane appeared to be radiantly happy.

"Jane, it's great to see you," I said. "Come into my office." She sat in a chair across the desk from me.

"Herb," she said excitedly. "Something wonderful has happened to me since I've seen you last.

"The Lord has saved me. I am born again."

To my sophisticated lawyer mind, her words had the ring of cheapness and vulgarity.

My poor sister, I thought. *She's got religion and got it bad! Why, she's a fanatic.*

"Herb," she continued. "I met some missionaries when I was down to visit Mom. They told me about Jesus Christ, who came not to condemn the world but to save it, not to take away life but to give it abundantly."

All the old cliches, I thought. But I had to admit Jane sounded convincing.

"Herb, it ended with me on my knees, confessing my sins and accepting Jesus Christ as my Savior. And Herb, Jesus Christ took away my sins and came into my heart, and it's simply wonderful."

The longer she talked the more uneasy I became. She used the words and phrases I'd heard before, but had never really listened to or understood.

"And Herb," she continued, "this is for you, too. Jesus is the Savior of the whole world. He died for your sins and He died for mine. For *all* men. He'll save you, too, if you'll let Him."

If sincerity could convert, Jane would have persuaded me to become a Christian that day.

"Herb," she pleaded, "I learned from the Bible that we all have sinned. We all need forgiveness from God. And do you know what? When He forgives, He gives you a new heart."

"Well, Jane, maybe this is all right for you, but it's not for me!" I said irritatedly. "And I don't want to waste your time or mine by going on."

Then, to direct the conversation elsewhere, I took a deep breath to calm myself and said, "By the way, how are Hedy and Mom?"

Jane got the point. We passed the rest of the time in small talk. I was glad when Jane said She had to leave.

But the words Jane had spoken stirred in my mind. It was as though she had turned on a phonograph within me. It was playing the same recording over and over. In my heart, I felt she was right, that I *did* need to trust God, to believe in Christ. Yet my intellect could not accept what she said. Her words were just that—words. There was no God, no supernatural Christ. Why should I believe such superstition?

Two weeks later, Jane visited our home. She arrived with a big black Bible tucked under her arm. I began with small talk apprehensive that she would again speak about "being saved by Jesus."

Unfortunately for me Gundhild had to go to the store for a few things. *I suppose I'll get a sermon again,* I thought.

Sure enough. Jane opened the big black Bible.

"I want to read a few words from the Scriptures to you, Herb."

Then she began. " 'Now there was a man of the Pharisees, named Nicodemus, a ruler of the Jews. This man came to Jesus by night and said to him, Rabbi, we know that you are a teacher come from God; for no one can do these signs that you do, unless God is with him. Jesus answered him, Truly, Truly, I say to you, unless one is born anew, he cannot see the King-dom of God.' "

Closing her Bible, she looked up at me.

"Herb, you are just like Nicodemus. He was an intelligent and decent man. A man of moral principles and a lawyer, just like you. But intelligence and ethics will not save you. Jesus said to Nicodemus, 'Except a man be born anew, he cannot see the Kingdom of God.' Herb, you've got to be born again. When I accepted Jesus as my Savior, that's what happened to me, and this is for you, too."

I shook my head in disgust.

"Herb, you have this lovely home. You are rich in so many ways and with many things, but these will not save you. There is only one way to God and eternal life. That way is to be born again."

I became infuriated. I stood up shouting.

"Jane, you've become fanatic! Leave me alone. I'm perfectly content the way I am and have decided to remain so. If you don't have anything else to talk about, then don't come to our home again!"

Jane was obviously stunned and hurt by my bluntness and show of temper. She put her Bible on the end table.

"Very well, Herb," she said softly, "let's talk about something else."

There was a long, awkward silence and words would not come for either of us. When Gundhild returned she carried on a conversation with Jane as she prepared and served lunch. After Jane left, she turned to me.

"What's wrong? What happened between Jane and you while I was gone?"

"Jane has gone nuts over religion," I snarled.

"She doesn't mean any harm," Gundhild counseled.

I grunted and half nodded, knowing she was right.

"Why did I become so angry?" I asked myself. "Jane seemed confused because I refused to be 'born again,' as though she had offered me a million dollars and I said, 'No thanks.' "

That night after getting to bed, I tossed and turned, recalling again and again her words, "Herb, you must be born again." The statement echoed in my mind.

What a stupid statement, I thought. *How can anyone possibly be born again?*

Then another thought occurred to me.

Maybe Jane is born again. Perhaps that's why she seems so happy and radiant. Whatever it is, I think she's right—I'm not born again. I'll probably end up in hell, if there is a hell, just as she says.

As a result of this sort of reasoning I became somewhat convicted about my life. But before I could act on these feelings, my logical mind took over.

It's just a delusion, pure and simple. Jane is suffering from some kind of a hallucination. She'll get over it and be herself soon.

But these thoughts did not reassure me. In fact, the simple statement, "You must be born again," could not be driven from my mind.

Jane's words continued to haunt me during the next few

months. It seemed as though every time I was alone, my conversation with Jane came to mind. I had to keep myself busy; I couldn't allow myself idle time or I'd be thinking again about her warning.

My mother, who had found it necessary to separate from my father because of his violence, had moved to Hollywood, California, shortly after I had enrolled at the University of Washington. She had written me an occasional letter through the years. But now she was writing more frequently and closing her letters with words like, "God will take care of you," or "I am always praying for you." This disturbed me, too.

"I am not sick. I don't need prayers," I said to myself. "Why is Mother praying for me?"

In one letter she wrote, "Every good lawyer knows his Bible, Herb. You should not neglect reading it. You can use it in pleading before a jury."

I had not learned that she, too, had become a Christian and that she was praying earnestly for the conversion of her entire family.

I was still stubborn and proud. I did not need God, if there was a God. I threw this answer out time and time again. Yet, after nights of sleeplessness and days of uncertainty, my stubborn unbelief was beginning to weaken.

6

I'M GOING TO FIND OUT
WHAT IT'S ALL ABOUT

Then one night I had a dream.

As I was driving down the main thoroughfare of Seattle with my wife and son in the front seat with me, a strange thing happened. We had just remarked about the unusually clear and bright day when suddenly, the quiet beauty of Seattle began to change. Violently, the buildings, bridges and homes began to wrench from their foundations and tumble down.

"It's an earthquake!" I screamed. Within seconds everything turned into a black, lifeless, chaotic mass of ruins. It was unreal and frightening. I cried, "Gundhild, this is a warning from God!" I tried to run away but couldn't move.

I awoke from sleep, my heart pounding. *It was a dream*—but so vivid that I was in a cold sweat. Shaken, I got up and paced the floor. As I did, the words of Jane again tormented my mind.

Up to this night my dreams had not been worth paying attention to, nor did they have meaning to me. But this dream experience was different. It left a deep, searing impression on my mind and memory.

In the morning I told Gundhild.

"I don't know about you, but I am going to church to find out what this is all about," I said.

"I'll go with you, Herb," Gundhild replied quietly.

We tried several churches—a Presbyterian church, the

Christian Church, a Methodist church, then a Missionary Alliance and a Pentecostal church. But I was uncomfortable. The services seemed strange. I didn't know the hymns and became embarrassed when I couldn't recite with the others.

My wife's fourteen-year-old niece, Marilyn Rolie, spoke to me one day. "Uncle Herb, I hear you are going to church. Why don't you visit our church?"

"Tell me which church and where, and we'll be there next Sunday," was my quick reply.

Marilyn's church, the Phinney Ridge Lutheran Church, was located in our part of the city. We met a couple our age in the foyer as we went in. They introduced themselves and were genuinely friendly. They even sat with us during the service. I felt very much "at home." My childhood contacts had been with the Lutheran church, so I was comfortable with the format of the worship service. The Rev. Rudolph Ofstedal, pastor, was a stately, blue-eyed, friendly Norwegian. When he preached, he had my attention completely. He did not read his sermon as others had done. Instead, he preached a logically developed sermon from notes in a conversational style. His illustrations clearly explained what the Bible meant to say. He was dealing with the problems of the heart, common to all men, using the Scriptures with telling effect. I felt immediately a strange Force at work in my heart and mind, wooing, convincing and convicting. It was as though God were *speaking to me* through this man.

The same friendly couple introduced us to the pastor at the door at the close of the service. His handshake and sincere interest in us seemed to say, "There is more that God has for you—come back again."

When we got home, I told Gundhild, "We have found our church."

"It seemed very nice indeed," she replied.

"From now on we will attend there regularly," I announced.

"It was a wonderful sermon. It was so down to earth. And the way the pastor explained the Bible I could understand all of it." she said.

Then I realized that was what intrigued me—the pastor's

understanding and knowledge of the Bible. Deep, deep down in my heart I now wanted to know what the Bible really taught. It was those words from the Bible which haunted me when Jane witnessed to me of her faith.

Later that week, we had a visit from the Rev. and Mrs. Ofstedal. They were cordial and friendly, and we were attracted to them at once.

Every Sunday thereafter we were at Phinney Ridge Lutheran Church. I enrolled Alton in Sunday School, and we went to the adult class taught by the pastor, and heard a comparative study of the Gospels. In this class on the life and ministry of Jesus Christ, I felt I was learning exactly what I wanted to know.

His sermons were hitting home, too, as he exposed the sins of the heart: lust, pride, anger, jealousy, hate, selfishness, and the like. I felt he was exposing my own heart every Sunday. He spoke about forgiveness of sins through Jesus Christ and explained the basis of that forgiveness through the atoning death of Jesus. At this point, however, I could not believe or accept this Gospel. I wondered if others really believed, or merely hoped or tried to believe. The pastor had such positive conviction as he spoke about trusting Christ, yet I wondered whether *he* really believed or was he kidding himself into believing it?

My logical and legal mind was saying, "How could a man take away my sins two thousand years ago even before I had committed them? And even if His death had been current, what legal disposition was His death for my sins? Even if I accepted the allegation that Jesus was both God and man, what could His death do to take away another man's guilt and sin and shame?"

The atoning death of Jesus Christ was an enigma to my mind. However, I agreed wholeheartedly with the moral righteousness which the Bible taught. I decided I would emulate that righteousness in my life. But I soon discovered experientially that I could not change my "inner man."

I was startled to learn that I had the very same experience as the Apostle Paul when he wrote, "I am carnal, sold under sin. I

38

do not understand my own actions. For I *do not do what I want,* but I do the very thing that I hate" (Romans 7:14-16). When the pastor used those very words in a sermon, I marvelled how the Apostle Paul, that great man of God, could write about the very same kind of an experience that I was having. I was discouraged at my attempts at changing my life. Upon hearing that Paul, too, had gone through a similar experience, and that Paul also had a trained legal and logical mind, I identified with him immediately.

I was asked if my family would like to join the church. Since it appeared that we had found our church home, I eagerly agreed. So, a few Sundays later, we went forward with others and became members.

About two months after we had started a regular attendance at Phinney Ridge Lutheran Church, the pastor announced that he had special classes for enquirers, "Twelve Lessons on How To Become a Lutheran." I discovered later that the lessons were really "How To Become a Christian."

Again I heard that message about Jesus and His atoning death. Gradually, things began to make sense. I did not know then that "faith comes from hearing, and hearing by the Word of Christ" (as Paul writes in Romans 10:17). But I was having that kind of an experience, slowly and surely, as I heard the truth of the Word of God from the pastor. Just as slowly, without real recognition on my part, my ideas of God, Jesus Christ, the Holy Spirit, heaven and hell began to change.

I took all twelve lessons, eagerly drinking in the truth of these spiritual things. Then I learned that the pastor was repeating the class for newcomers. I enrolled to take those lessons all over again. My spirit hungered for something I could not quite pin down.

By the end of those six months, I had a conviction that the message concerning Christ was true. Yet, I also knew something was still missing. My sinful heart was plaguing me. Terrible guilt feelings overwhelmed me. I knew by now that I could not change myself through self-discipline and will power. Outwardly, I could make a good show, but I knew by then that God doesn't look at outward appearances, but at the heart. I

39

knew I could fool men, but I could not fool God. So, even though I was absorbing Bible knowledge like a sponge, I knew that in my heart I was still sinful and lost in the sight of God. I was a church member. But that made no difference to the Lord. He knew what the real Herb Mjorud was like.

One night I decided to write a letter to my mother. I had been inwardly distressed about my hopeless condition. My soul struggled for true righteousness without success. I told her my inner thoughts, thinking perhaps she could give me some advice. She seemed to have discovered the source of peace of mind. I had told Gundhild I had to stay up and think things through and would come to bed late. Knowing I wanted to be alone, she went to bed.

So I began my letter.

Dear Mother,

I don't know why I'm sharing these thoughts with you. But you know I have been down many blind alleys in my former way of living. I've been searching for success and satisfaction. In my youth, it was basketball. In college, it was rowing. These achievements were fine as sports, but not as a way of life. Then, through your loving encouragement, I began my life as a lawyer. Yet, though I had high ideals and noble purposes, this vocation itself is not a way of life. I can't find satisfaction or the answers to life's deep mysteries. There has to be more to life.

Why was I born? What is the meaning of life? I've been attending church regularly. We have a good pastor who preaches the Bible. I want to say, "I finally have become a Christian," but the thought in my mind makes me heavy hearted. I know that I honestly cannot write that statement. There is still something missing.

In despair I dropped my head into my hands. All I could see in myself was sin and utter failure in life. I began to pray! Not repeating the Lord's prayer this time, but calling upon God to express my inner thoughts.

"O God, I am a sinner, forgive me, forgive me, forgive me!"

The weight of all my wrongs choked the words in my throat. Weeping, I began confessing these sins, starting in childhood. I recalled when I nearly drowned at age twelve and remembered the flashback of those childhood sins. I confessed everything I could remember all through my life. It took a long time!

"O God, You have to forgive me . . . not only for what I have done, but for what I *am*. I am a sinful man, a slave to sin. No matter how hard I try, I can't change. In fact, I'm getting worse . . . . Lord, I *do* believe in Jesus Christ. I believe just as Your Word says, that He was with You to create the worlds, that He was God and yet became a man like us. I also believe that Jesus lived the perfect life and died on the cross. He died for *me!* Yes, Lord, I believe! I believe!"

Suddenly, I felt I was in the presence of the Lord Jesus Christ. My eyes were still closed, my head in my hands, but I had the sensation that bright light surrounded me. I dared not look up, lest I should see Him. There was both fear and elation in that experience. My guilt feelings were drained away, and the peace and love of God seemed to flood over me. My inner being began to warm. Nerve endings in my skin began to tingle. I began to weep with joy.

I could hardly speak a word, but I began saying, "O God, my Father, thank You, thank You, thank You!" and this over and over again. I awoke Gundhild to tell her of my experience.

The next morning, I called my sister Jane. She had stayed away from me since I had so rudely offended her when she tried to share her faith with me. When she answered the phone, I merely said, "Jane, this is Herb."

Without hesitating, she cried, "Herb, you've been born again!"

"Who told you?"

"I can hear it in your voice," was her knowing reply.

That morning I felt like I *was* reborn into a new world. I went outside before breakfast where a light rain was falling. I held my face to the sky and welcomed the fresh mist upon my skin. It seemed as though each drop were a touch from God Himself. The singing of the birds sounded like doxologies of praise. The whole of creation seemed to sing, "We are a part of all that the Lord is doing." I had finally come in tune with God and was sensitive to all His goodness and creation.

Church services became a new experience, too. The pastor still spoke about the sins of the heart, but when he talked about forgiveness through the atoning death of Jesus Christ, I could say "Amen" in my heart and rejoice as a forgiven soul, a new man. This joy continued for months.

Shortly after my conversion, my pastor came to me.

"Herb, I'd like you to teach a Sunday School class."

"But, Pastor, I'm not qualified to teach others. I'm such a beginner myself."

He acted as though he didn't hear me and put the materials in my hands.

"The Lord is your sufficiency, Herb."

Had I known this was a stepping stone to full-time ministry, the decision would have been far more grave. It was already difficult.

One part of me was recoiling and saying, "I must be careful of getting too religious. What will people say, especially my lawyer friends? Besides, I don't really have time to do this." I knew I could turn down this call and justify my decision by my lack of Biblical knowledge, my inexperience in teaching.

But there was something else saying within me, "I want to serve the Lord and make some kind of a contribution to His kingdom." I knew the pastor's statement, "The Lord is your sufficiency," was the truth.

I smiled and gave the pastor my answer: "I'll give it my best try."

Later, at our annual church meeting, I was dumbfounded to be elected a deacon. Again came the conflict of doubting: "Who am I to lead others when I have so much to learn myself?"

When I expressed my doubts to my pastor, he said, "Mjorud, when the Lord calls you, He also supplies the wisdom and the power. God *has* called you. He knows you better than you know your own qualifications."

I had nothing more to say. By faith I took these additional responsibilities, believing the Lord would help.

"Lord, if you are going to use me, You will have to train me. I need to know more of Your Word. I haven't had the advantages of others who have grown up in the church. Lord, please open up a way that I may learn the Scriptures," I prayed.

7

"CAN I TRUST
YOU FOR MIRACLES?"

The Lord has His own way of answering prayer. He makes it another step in obedience. The Lutheran Bible Institute in Seattle was in its second year as an extension of the parent school in Minneapolis.

Then one night I heard the Rev. Eugene Stime, dean of this school, preach. He spoke so directly and pointedly from the Bible that I was transfixed. I longed to take instruction from such a knowledgeable teacher. I wondered as I heard him whether it would be possible to do so.

My law partner, Warren Ploeger, who had been in the Naval Reserves, was serving somewhere in the Pacific. Alone in our law offices, I felt obligated to build up our practice in his absence. *So,* I reasoned, *it won't be practical for me to leave the office, even for a month.*

At the close of that special service, Bertil Stromberg, a Canadian who had come to Christ from a background and experience like mine, and I were talking.

"Herb, I'm going down and register for some classes in this new school tomorrow. I've got three months to wait for my American citizenship papers and can afford to spend my time profitably in the study of God's Word."

"I wish I could do the same but my practice would suffer terribly if I did," I said.

"But you could take the first two classes in the morning at eight and nine o'clock," he countered, "and still be in your office a little after ten."

"Really? Maybe I'll go down with you in the morning," I said rather cautiously.

I wrestled in prayer about the matter the night before registration. The Lord seemed to say, "You asked for the opportunity for training in My Word. I am opening a door for you. Step out in faith and have no fear."

But I had all manner of reservations. Logically, I had weighed the many pros and cons. The cons far outweighed the pros. To go to a Bible school was against my better judgment. Many would not understand and ridicule me. Yet deep within me was this assurance from God that this was His will. The decision was difficult. I was confronted with a logical, obvious choice but was being "told" to reject it. By faith I had to learn dependence, total dependence.

I was about to understand experientially something that was written of Jesus, "He learned obedience by the things that He *suffered.*" Obedience to the Lord involves this inner warfare between the new Christ-life and one's alter ego, the old self-life. Paul wrote of this inner struggle in Galatians 5:17, "For the desires of the flesh (*the old self-life*) are against the spirit (*the new Christ-life*), and the desires of the spirit are against the flesh; for *these are opposed to each other,* to prevent you from doing what you would."

The more I thought about it, the more confused I became. However, I came to grips with the matter by praying, "Lord, You have made this opportunity. I fully believe You are saying, 'Step out in faith and have no fear.' So in spite of the consequences, I am going to enroll in Bible school classes tomorrow morning that I might take hold of Your Word. This is my decision; help me in my weakness. Amen."

I had peace. The wrestling in my mind was over. Still, adverse thoughts hovered over me. My natural feelings gave vent to the desire to reconsider the decision, but I held firm.

The next morning I drove to the Lutheran Bible Institute with the resolve that I would enroll for two classes in the morning, at eight and nine o'clock. Bert was already there and was registering for a full course load. He took four classes from eight until noon, Monday through Friday. Trusting God, I also registered for all classes.

I decided I would practice law in the afternoons!

But I got so absorbed and involved in studying the Word of God that I didn't even find time to get to my office in the afternoons.

Another attorney came one day and asked to rent my law partner's office in his absence and I consented. After this, I found myself turning one case after another over to him. It wasn't long before my entire practice was his.

At the end of the first quarter, I felt God wanted me to learn more, so I enrolled for the rest of the two-year course.

During my two years at Bible school, I constantly felt guilty because I wasn't in my law office building up the practice. I wasn't concerned about myself, but felt the obligation to my law partner who was on military duty overseas and expecting me to keep the practice going. But most of my time was spent either in study of the Bible or in service to my church. The pastor and I had become close friends. We chatted often together over various aspects of the Christian faith.

"I'm beginning to get a feel for your deep burden to reach souls for Jesus Christ and to build the Kingdom of God," I told him one day.

He seemed to be in deep thought on this matter. He replied slowly.

"Herb, there is so much we can and must do. Our church is packed on Sundays, but I still see fields 'ripe unto harvest.' I'm convinced that, under God, I am a harvester. But, Herb, what about you?

"Do you know there are over fifty thousand people in Seattle with a Lutheran background who are never in church on Sunday morning?" He sipped from his cup of coffee as I thought about that. "They are no more precious in God's sight than thousands of others in Seattle, but the fact they are Lutheran in background *does* give us an 'in' to reach them for Christ."

I was puzzled. "What can we do locally to reach some of them? Should we do some comprehensive advertising to bring them into the church?"

"No, advertising may help some, but it takes prayer and hard work to reach souls for Christ. Herb, you ought to know that in fishing you don't set your nets, then put up a sign which says, 'Here's a place to get caught.' You have to go out to the banks and set your nets where the fish are. Remember, the word *Gospel* has the word '*go*' in it. We must go to the people and confront them personally."

"But fifty thousand is a lot of people," I said.

Out of our conversation came other sessions where we talked about confronting men and women with the claims of Jesus Christ. Then came a program for canvassing the entire north side of Seattle with a follow-up of visitation evangelism, two by two. Almost without knowing it, I had become an assistant pastor.

I was thrilled with actual ministry in the Kingdom. I was especially excited doing the follow-up work, where we went by two's into the homes and spoke to prospects about our own faith in Jesus Christ.

The results were amazing. So many new people began attending our church that we had to hold two services every Sunday morning! The pastor's classes were filled. People were seeking answers as I had done a few years before. Our entire congregation was renewed into vigorous spiritual vitality through this active participation of so many of its members.

We put our evangelism program in operation, and I was busy in visitation, teaching a Sunday School class, and as superintendent of the adult department of Sunday School.

With the daily study of the Word in the morning classes at the Bible school, plus my involvement in the evangelism program of our church, I had little time for tne practice of law. For some time I had been releasing one case after another to Stuart Nielsen, the attorney who had rented my partner's office. Since my commercial fishing gave me an ample income, I was glad to see Nielsen's practice growing steadily. But I did regret I was not doing the same for the sake of my partner.

Yet I was enjoying my full involvement in the Lord's work. I was thrilled with the study of God's Word and exhilarated with my soul winning efforts. Nothing before had ever brought me such satisfaction—not sports, not fishing, not practicing law. This may explain why I couldn't stop my studies after just one quarter. My thought was that there would be ample time in the future to practice law, but for the moment I had to lay hold of God's Word and do His Work. Nothing seemed more important than this outreach in our local community.

While I believed I was training myself to become a busy layman in the church, God had other plans for me! During my second year at the Bible school, God began speaking to me through His Word. Every time I came across words like, "Come ye after Me and I will make you to become a *fisher of men*," the words seemed addressed directly to me personally. And an inner voice followed the question with these words: "Herb, are you willing?"

As an assignment in one class, we were asked to write a theme on "Discipleship in the Kingdom," taking our directives from the Bible. With every word I wrote and with every verse I quoted from the Bible on discipleship, came the inner question, "How about you? Are you willing?"

I would shrug this off by saying, "But, Lord, I'm here training to become an active layman, not a missionary or a preacher." Yet, I couldn't shake the sense that God was calling me to serve full-time in His Kingdom. I had a secret fear. I knew the only door open to a Bible school graduate was the mission field. I didn't *want* to be a missionary! I didn't want to change culture, language and country at the age of 37. But there was no escaping Christ's call.

As the weeks wore on, my heart became heavy. I began to see that Jesus Christ was not yet Lord of my life. I struggled over my unwillingness to tell Him, "Yes, no matter what!"

I argued with God. "But Lord, I've been trained as a lawyer. With you leading me, I will certainly succeed in my chosen profession as a lawyer. And I will be a devoted layman in Your work."

But I knew inwardly that the Lord was not accepting my

words. They were *my words* and *not His will.* I knew I had to face up to the burden the Lord had laid upon me. I paced the floor, wondering whether I had the courage to really go all the way and say, "Jesus, I acknowledge You as Lord of my life, no matter what this means." I rolled the phrase around in my mind. It was easy to say. But I knew I wasn't ready or able to do it. One night, I went into my bedroom to be alone.

"Lord, give me the courage to be willing to do Your will, no matter what it means," I prayed. "Jesus, You have saved me, given me a new life, and blessed me in every way. I come to You now, in the best way I know how. Take my life, my all. I give everything to You. I lay before You my law practice, my family, my fishing business, and my home. Everything I am and have is Yours. I am willing to do Your will, *no matter what!* Even if You want me to become a missionary!"

Suddenly my burden lifted. I knew the Lord had accepted my consecration. It was done! I had surrendered my life. I concluded that this meant to leave my law practice, sell my lovely home, and burn all my bridges so Christ could really be Lord in my life.

I had recurring fears about my decision. Once again God was asking me to ignore logic and "sense." But, after all, I had been trained as an attorney. Why would the Lord have me waste those years in getting an education that I wouldn't need if He wanted me to be a missionary?

I didn't relate my decision fully to Gundhild right away. I simply told her I had dedicated my life to the Lord and He had given me inner peace. I knew my decision involved her and her life. I wondered what she'd say when I told her I was quitting the law practice and selling all to follow Christ!

After making my decision to serve the Lord full-time I thought that I'd go directly to some mission field from Bible school graduation. But I learned that mission boards were only taking seminary trained and ordained men into this ministry. That meant I had to do further study—spend three more years at Luther Theological Seminary to get a license to preach. Three years of seminary training! How formidable they seemed. I felt I'd gone to school half a lifetime already—four years of college, three years of law school, two years of Bible school, and now three years more of seminary!

I prayed earnestly about this. "Lord, do You really want me to go to seminary?" The answer I received was, "Yes."

Now, I couldn't postpone telling Gundhild. We'd have to sell the house, move to St. Paul, Minnesota, and enroll at Luther Theological Seminary as God was leading me to do. When I did tell her, she amazed me.

"I knew this a long time ago. I have complete peace about it, too."

What I had struggled through, she knew by intuition! The Lord seemed always to be one step ahead of me in everything. Then one evening, I received an unexpected telephone call from my law partner.

"Herb! This is Warren Ploeger. I've just returned from the service and already am discharged. I'm in town!"

I got a sick feeling in the pit of my stomach.

"Warren, how good to hear from you. Can we meet at our law offices in the morning? There's a lot I have to tell you."

I was apprehensive at the thought of meeting Warren. Not only had I failed to build up a law practice for him to step into, but now, because of my plans to enter the ministry, I had to ask him for a dissolution of our partnership. I anticipated a very difficult embarrassing meeting. But I gave this problem to the Lord, too.

When we met the next morning, I found Warren cordial and friendly, as always. After passing courtesies and catching up on family news, Warren shifted the subject to my commercial fishing. Then he appeared embarrassed.

"Herb . . . there's no easy way to say this. But, well, much has happened these past few years. Herb, I have been offered a wonderful position with the Northern Pacific Railway Company in their law department. I'd be working in Real Estate Law, and you know how this has been my specialty. I feel elated about the prospects of working there. But . . . to do this, we'd have to dissolve our partnership."

I was almost speechless. The Lord again had prepared everything, even to supplying my partner with a fine job!

50

I told Warren my plans for the ministry and the seminary training, and let him know that I wanted to dissolve the partnership, too. He was astonished at my decision to change professions and my willingness to burn bridges to follow my convictions.

"There's a great need, Herb," he said soberly. "The moral and spiritual condition of our country is receding since the war. I am sure you'll do well in the ministry."

Warren volunteered to sell our books and office furniture. He made all the arrangements for the dissolution of the partnership. God paved the way once more so that this was done quickly and easily.

Now it came time to trust God again.

Our home had been up for sale for many months, but we had no prospective buyers. We had a van come to our home about three weeks before our departure to St. Paul. The truck left with all our furniture and personal belongings. But our house was not sold as yet and there was still no prospect as far as we knew.

We made this a matter of special prayer. "Lord, you know the way we are taking, and this house must be sold."

Two more weeks went by. There was but one week before we had to leave for St. Paul. The real estate agent called and said he had a prospect who wanted to see the house. When he brought the young man in, the latter said, "Can I see your bedrooms?" We had one unusually large bedroom and thought this might deter a sale. I led them into our master bedroom anyway.

"This is exactly the house we are looking for," the man told the agent. "We've looked at many houses, but our four poster will only fit in this bedroom!" Within twenty-four hours, the deal was completed.

After arriving in St. Paul, we purchased another home near Luther Seminary where I expected to study theology for the next three years. I kept ownership in the "Ellie IV" with plans to fish during the summer vacations to finance this further pursuit in higher education.

"Lord, can I trust you for miracles here, too?" I wondered.

8

A MIRACULOUS CATCH OF FISH

I had burned the bridges behind me. I had no law practice or regular income to pay my expenses through Bible school and seminary. The "insecurity" of such a foolish action should have made me nervous. But the Lord continued to give me peace.

As a non-practicing lawyer, I had no cash reserves. But I did have an alternative—commercial fishing. I had earned money fishing to finance my schooling since high school. I could always go back to three months of fishing in the Pacific to keep us solvent. I gave the matter to God.

I was still a half owner of the "Ellie IV," the fifty-foot salmon and tuna troller. She weighed twenty-six gross tons and had a fish-hold capacity of twelve tons of iced fish. Harold Beck, a fellow Christian who lived in Seattle where the boat was moored, made all the pre-season preparations—repainting, rigging gear, and outfitting the "Ellie IV."

When my first year of Bible school was over June 1, I went fishing with Harold for the summer.

Harold became my deckhand. We stowed provisions and gear aboard the "Ellie IV" for a two-week trip. We filled our tanks with diesel fuel, and took on eight tons of crushed ice for the fish-hold. My wife, Gundhild, and Harold's wife, Ruth, and our two boys gathered with us in the galley. We asked the Lord to bless our fishing ventures that summer and committed each other to God's care—little knowing the adventure that awaited us.

We left the docks at Lake Union in Seattle, went through the locks into Puget Sound, and by nightfall were chugging out the Straits of Juan De Fuca. Our plans were to fish for king salmon off the west coast of Vancouver Island in the open ocean. There was always much work to be done enroute to the fishing banks, rigging gear, and shining spoons (lures). With the "iron mike" (an automatic steering device) engaged to hold the set course, both Harold and I could be kept busy. Each of us took a two-hour watch in the wheelhouse. We were well-trained seamen, capable of all the work, including navigation—reading charts or plotting courses. We planned to travel through the night until we came to some fishing bank.

At nightfall, we tuned our shortwave radio to listen to the ship band. We could hear from other fishing boats to learn where the fishing was good after we had cleared the Straits of Juan De Fuca. But the news was bad. Fishing had been poor everywhere. We decided to try "Forty Mile," a bank so called because it was forty miles from Cape Flattery, the northwestern extremity of Washington.

The "Ellie IV" cruised at eight knots. Some fifteen hours out of Seattle, we sighted the fleet. Two hundred fishing vessels were trolling on the Forty Mile. We arrived at the banks about six o'clock in the morning and began preparations for actual fishing. Harold lowered our fishing poles, two forty-four-footers at midship from the mainmast, and two thirty-two-footers extending forward at a forty-five degree angle from the foremast.

Since we often had to fish in rough seas, everything was rigged to withstand those pressures. The fishing poles were well secured with wire guide cables up and down, fore and aft. They remained steady in the heaviest of weather.

"Slow to a two-knot speed!" I called to Harold in the wheelhouse.

We held to this speed as we trolled for salmon. We set out our six lines with four and five leaders per line with a lure on each leader. Our main lines were one-eighth-inch stainless steel cable, twelve-hundred-pound test. These were wound on a winch called a "gurdie" and were easily manipulated in and out with a braking clutch. Each line was weighted with single leads. The fore lines were weighted with a forty-five-pound found-molded lead. The other four with twenty- and fifteen-pound leads. This brought the lines deep into the water and enabled us to catch fish even at a depth of one hundred fathoms (six feet to a fathom).

Leaders were snapped on the lines at intervals of five fathoms, or thirty feet. The leaders were from three to five fathoms in length with a lure at the end of each. We had "tag lines" from each pole. When we came to the desired depth for fishing, these would be snapped onto the stainless steel line, then the pole would catch the entire weight of that line.

When a fish hit a lure, the pole would shake, indicating the strike. Then we would engage the clutch on the gurdie for that line and begin to wind in the fish. First, the tag line would be unsnapped, then the leaders likewise as the line came in. When we came to a leader with a fish on it, the clutch would be disengaged and put into the braking position to hold the line. The fish would then be played from the leader. Playing these large fish took skill and experience. We used a gaffhook in landing salmon—first stunning the fish expertly on the head, then using the hook to hoist them aboard. We landed the fish from a trolling hatch in the aft of the boat, which was about three feet in depth and allowed us to come close to the fish.

On the Forty Mile bank, the depth of the water was uniform, varying between thirty-five and forty fathoms. We set our lines and were fishing that day near the bottom.

"Harold, the water's unusually brown. This is a good sign," I called out. (The brown color was from plankton, the feed for herring. Herring, in turn, was feed for salmon.) "There're also many gulls feeding on the bank. Those are good signs, too."

But as we trolled along, there was little action. It was over an hour before we landed our first salmon. By nine o'clock in the evening we had caught just six small salmon. We signaled to other boats with the show of fingers to indicate our catch. We learned from their signals that their catches were small, too—from four to ten fish.

The next day was no better.

"What's wrong, Herb?" asked Harold.

"There are simply too many boats fishing this bank for the quantity of fish available," I replied.

By eight a.m. we had caught only three fish. We had begun fishing at daybreak, which was two-thirty in the morning this far north. This was not good.

I went into the pilot house, took down the chart table, and studied it. "Where can we go to find better fishing," I asked myself. I was nervous and upset. I had been in Bible school for nine months with no income during that time. I had let my law practice go entirely into the hands of another. My cash reserves were low. Expenses both at home and for the boat were high and now, no fish!

I began to pray. "Lord, surely somewhere in this large ocean of Yours there must be more fish to be caught than we are catching here."

I paused and I heard a voice inwardly say, "Cast your gear to the right side of your boat and you will find some."

I was startled. Where did this advice come from?

The Lord had said something similar to Peter. Before I could, in my mind, wrestle over what I had heard, I looked on the chart to the right of our present position and noted a deep trough on the ocean floor, about five miles long and two miles wide. It was sixty fathoms in depth compared to the thirty-five to forty fathoms on our present bank and the surrounding ocean bottom picture. This trough was about four miles distant from our present position.

I took out my parallel rulers and plotted a course to that trough. Then I disengaged the "Iron Mike" and spun the steering wheel until the compass showed we were headed on a course due northeast from our present position. I re-engaged "Iron Mike" on course to the trough and went aft to tell Harold of my plans.

"I believe I have a clue from the Lord. Uh . . . we'll try fishing about four miles northeast of here."

I dared not tell him the whole truth of the matter. But since there weren't many fish on the Forty Mile, he didn't voice any opposition to the move.

We kept our lines in the water, trolling all the way. It would take several hours to reach our destination. However, there wasn't one bite from a fish all along that run.

Harold came over when we stopped.

"The water's really a green color," he observed. We both knew that that was *not* a good sign. There were no gulls, no feeding herring. Everything I had learned as an experienced fisherman was telling me that the Lord had given me a bum steer.

I drank coffee and paced the deck. I felt foolish. Had I really heard a voice from the Lord? Or had it been merely my own inner thoughts?

I had ample time to ponder my experience. My mind became confused. I wondered if I had been tricked with my own imagination or wishful thinking.

I recalled then how Peter was told by the Lord, "Launch out into the deep and let down your nets for a catch of fish." I had rapport with Peter's thoughts. He also knew as an experienced fisherman that you don't fish with his type of nets in broad daylight in clear-water lakes. Peter knew every fishing spot on that lake and every one of them was on the banks—not out in the deep middle. No doubt, Peter was worrying about what his fishing partners, Andrew and John, would say. If he threw out the nets which already had been washed, mended and ready for that evening's try, he would be the laughing stock of the whole fishing community.

Peter had been in a quandry, and so was I.

I wanted to turn back to the fleet or pick up my lines and run west and try another bank. Everything I knew about commercial fishing was against this present venture. I went back into the trolling hatch and pulled a bow line to the tag line, then unsnapped the tag line so that I could sound the depth of the water. I was hoping that somehow we could reach this deep earlier than scheduled so that we could get the thing over with. But upon doing so, I found the depth to be still about thirty-five fathoms.

I went into the galley, took down my Bible, and read about Peter: first, his experience with Jesus on the Sea of Galilee, then his later experience when the Lord, in the early morning sunlight on the beach, told him, "Cast your nets to the *right side of the boat* you will catch some." Peter caught a record haul.

I tried to pray but my mind was a jumble of confusion. No doubt Peter was thinking, *Lord, you might know how to preach, but You surely don't know the first thing about net fishing.*

Yet he said to Jesus, "Lord, we fished all night and caught nothing, but at Your word I will cast out the net."

Somehow, I had to trust God, too. I determined not to go out on deck again until we had run the time for reaching that deep trough.

When the time had come, I went out and lowered a line. It went to sixty fathoms! We were in the deep trough! I hoisted the line, clamped on the tag line, and as quickly as the line was taut, the pole began to shake. I studied the shaking. I wanted to be sure it wasn't the lead bouncing on the bottom. But my experience told me that we had hooked a large salmon! I lowered the starboard bow line and as soon as that pole took the weight of the line, it began to shake! We had hooked another fish! We lowered the dog lines on floats dragged thirty fathoms to the rear. Then we lowered the midship lines. Before we got to hoisting that first line, all the poles were shaking. It was apparent that we had fish on every line!

I hauled in the first line. There wasn't one large king salmon, but *two,* each weighing about thirty pounds!

Our first catches were four times the size of the small fish we had caught the day before. We worked the trolling hatch, I on the port side and Harold on the starboard. Shouting, singing and puffing, within the first hour we had landed over twenty large king salmon, running from fifteen to forty pounds. They were unbelievable beauties!

There is no more beautiful fish in the ocean than the king salmon. It bears its regal name for a reason. Its green-blue back shades into a silvery white on the bottom, a sprinkling of irridescent colors, and with red and gold causing the scales to sparkle like opal in a noonday sun.

We trolled in that deep trough all the rest of that day. By nightfall we had an excellent haul of king salmon. After the fish were gutted and cleaned, we put them into the fish-hold, packing them with crushed ice. We always counted the fish we caught as we put them in the fish-hold.

"Here's the last ones, Harold," I said, lowering them into the ice bins. "Let's see . . . that's one hundred and forty-nine . . . one hundred and fifty . . . one hundred and fifty-one . . . one hundred and fifty-two . . . one hundred fifty-three."

One hundred and fifty-three! The number made the hair stand up on the back of my neck.

"How many fish did Peter catch that morning with Jesus?" I asked, knowing full well the answer. I had just read the account from my Bible.

"I don't know—why? You want me to find out?" he asked.

I nodded, and Harold went into the galley for his New Testament. He found the right place. His eyes widened.

"Herb! Peter caught exactly one hundred fifty-three fish, too!"

Not only did we get a large catch of extra big fish, but we caught a "miracle" number—one hundred fifty-three. Harold began singing, "Praise God from whom all blessings flow," and I joined him, my faith bolstered by this act of obedience to what seemed a futile and ridiculous action.

It was about eleven p.m. We dropped anchor right there on our fishing spot. The sea was calm, and there was a gentle westerly breeze. The skies were clear; and stars were out. The moon was shimmering upon the sea to give our singing a setting more appropriate than the most stately of cathedrals.

I remembered that when John, the fishing partner of Peter, saw the great number of fish they caught when the Lord gave His command, he shouted, "It is the Lord." Likewise, when we counted one hundred fifty-three huge fish, we shouted with all our hearts, "It is the Lord."

In my closing prayer that night, I said, "Thank You, Lord, for this wonderful catch of fish. Forgive me for the doubts I had on the way over. But, Lord, can I always count on the kind of guidance You gave me today? In my fishing? In my law practice?" There was something real in His leading—call it intuition, a hunch—no, it was much more than that. But I recalled vividly how God had come to my mind and thought patterns—again, not in a logical way, but through a totally illogical experience in order to prove my faith through obedience.

At two a.m. the alarm clock went off. It isn't easy to get going after just three hours of sleep and the hard work of the preceding day. But in fishing, time is always of the essence. Harold put the water on for coffee. I went to the engine room to oil and start the diesel engine. Then Harold went to the foredeck to wind the anchor cable on the power winch. In only a matter of minutes the boat was moving at two knots again, and we were lowering our lines to take advantage of a bite at daybreak. We were not disappointed. Before the coffee had brewed, we had landed several large and beautiful king salmon.

"Peter had nothing on us," I remarked. "Look at the size of these beauties!"

The day proved a fisherman's dream. There was not another boat around, the weather was perfect, and we had another banner catch—one hundred sixty-seven fish. We continued in that same deep trough for seven days.

On the eighth day, the fleet found us and learned of our success. But by now the good fishing lasted only for a few hours in the morning. Then the currents changed. Soon there were such undercurrents that it was impossible to fish the deep water any longer. By that time, however, we had caught over one thousand large king salmon! Our crushed ice was almost gone. We decided to leave so that we could make the morning auction for the fish buyers in Seattle.

We brought into Seattle the largest catch of troll-caught king salmon *in over a decade!* We hauled our catch on the "big board" and various fish buyers bid for it. As the prices changed, the auction agent erased the old bids and put up the new. Our catch was bid upon briskly and brought a good price. My deckhand and I netted *over one thousand three hundred dollars each* for our first week at sea that summer!

Days later, in a harbor to wait out a storm, we talked with several Canadian fishermen over coffee. The conversation was about our banner trip which everyone had heard about by this time. They shook their heads.

"It's really quite amazing," one old salt said. "That trough in which you found such great fishing has been tried and tried. No one has ever pulled king salmon out of it. All anyone's ever caught there are dogfish and skates!"

Through the years, we learned from other fishermen that that pattern had never changed. King salmon were *never* found in that trough again.

9

OBEDIENCE IS NECESSARY

Now I began to seek guidance from the Lord on every trip. The Lord, in turn, led us to where the fish were. God was running my business. The "Ellie IV" was the talk of the fishing fleet. It became common knowledge that I was always found where the best fishing was. There were many bonanza trips. The question in every skipper's mind when seeking a likely bank to fish was, "Where is Herb Mjorud?"—for when he found our boat, he found good fishing!

But I also had problems to face. I discovered that faith was also a matter of discipline.

While at the Bible school for my second year of study, I was criticized for ignoring the needs of my family. The critic was my father, John Mjorud, who owned the fine troller, "Cape Ommaney." Dad was an ace fisherman. He'd start the fishing season in early March. After every trip, he would phone Gundhild and tell her, "Herb has gone just too far with this religion bit!

"Everybody knows he left off practicing law," he said on one occasion, "and has thrown away his education. He has that big boat there, tied to the docks doing nothing. Doesn't he realize he has a family to support? Let him know that I told you—he's not tending to his business. He's neglecting his family. Everybody is talking about him and what they are saying is not good!"

"Don't worry about Herb," my wife assured Father. "He knows what he's doing, and the Lord takes care of us."

"Yes, the Lord feeds the birds, but they don't keep sitting in their nests!" was Dad's quick reply.

"Herb will be fishing after he graduates from Bible school and will fish all summer as usual. God will help him supply our needs," Gundhild replied.

It was the first of June before school was over. Soon Harold Beck, my deckhand, and I were preparing for our second fishing season together.

"Where are you going to try for fish this time?" Harold asked as we stowed away our groceries and made ready for our first trip.

"I don't know where we'll go, but God will direct us," was my reply. We prayed together with our two wives and my sons. As we prayed for guidance, the answer that I received seemed to be, "I will let you know as you go along."

When we came out of Puget Sound and were abreast of Port Townsend, we were in need of directions, whether to go west, out the Straits of Juan de Fuca, or north, via the Inside Passage to Hecate Straits.

We met a troller headed back to Seattle. One of the men aboard her was signaling to us.

"We have just come from Hecate Straits and have about six thousands pounds aboard," Joe Rockom, the skipper, informed us.

"I have never seen that place with better signs for many a year," his son, Willis, shouted to us. "We caught our trip mainly on the Horse Shoe Ground but when we came over Goose Island bank, it was covered with blackbirds, with feed everywhere. We set out our gear and trolled across the bank and caught five slugs (large king salmon)!"

The Lord had given us His guidance "along the way," as He had said He would. We thanked our benefactors and set our course for the Inside Passage. This meant traveling day and night for forty-eight hours, navigating the narrow channels on the inside of Vancouver Island in British Columbia. When we came to Queen Charlotte Sound, we set a course for the Goose

Island bank, forty miles out to sea southwest of Goose Island.

At midnight we stopped our boat, sounded and found the desired depth of water, forty fathoms, and dropped our anchor. There were no other boats on the bank.

"We've anchored out boat over a school of salmon," I said to Harold. "I just know it. And we have them all to ourselves! Let's set our alarm for five o'clock and 'oversleep' a bit so we'll be rested for tomorrow."

The next morning our gear was out by five fifteen a.m. A half hour later, we landed our first king salmon, a thirty-five-pounder. We began tacking back and forth across that bank, going about two miles on each tack. We caught five or six large salmon on every tack. By evening we had landed one hundred and ten large kings, averaging about twenty pounds each! We had over a ton of fish aboard. That is great fishing!

The following day, the fishing was even better. *We doubled our catch!* On the third day, we caught around twenty-five fish by eight o'clock, then twenty or more trollers approached us from the west. By the time they had made one sweep over the bank, the fish had either moved or were caught. During the next five or six hours, there wasn't a single bite.

I went into the pilot house and pulled out the Hecate Strait chart, plotting courses to the Ramsey Island bank, ninety miles due west, or to the Horse Shoe bank, one hundred and five miles west by north. I prayed and asked the Lord what to do.

"Pull your gear and go for Ramsey Island bank," was the inner word.

By leaving at that hour, we could run all night and be on the Ramsey Island bank by daybreak. We pulled in our gear; revved up the motor to our cruising speed of eight knots. The fleet did the same and followed us.

The next morning we came to the Ramsey Island bank. Another fleet of thirty or so trollers already was fishing that bank. We set out our gear and trolled north across that bank and didn't get a bite. Some trollers we passed signaled to catching three to five fish.

Disappointed, I went into the pilot house.

"Lord," I said, "I'm minded to pull up my gear and head for

the Horse Shoe Grounds!" And the word I received was, "Get going."

I wondered why the Lord hadn't told me to go directly to this ground, but I was soon to learn why. We had sixteen miles to travel at full speed, so after a two-hour run, we slowed the boat to trolling speed and set out our gear. I sounded and found we were in sixty fathoms of water, so I knew we had overrun the bank.

"I didn't allow for the incoming tide," I told Harold, "so we'll have to turn south, back to the bank."

One boat had followed us. The man set out his gear when we did but kept going north in that deep water about a mile farther than we did before he had turned. Apparently the tide was running rather swiftly, for it took much longer than expected before we came back to the bank—over an hour or so.

Our companion boat was equipped with radio telephone. Its skipper called one of the trollers left behind at the Ramsey Island bank. We were tuned in on our radio over the ship band, which was usually on to pick up fishing news all hours of the day.

"I haven't had one strike here on the Horse Shoe bank," he bewailed. "I have fished here over an hour and it looks very bleak. Herb Mjorud hasn't caught anything either because I have had my glasses on him constantly. How are things over there?"

"Picking up. We've caught sixteen big ones," was the reply from the boat on the Ramsey Island bank. "And the other boats are doing about the same."

"That's better than we've got. I'm pulling up and heading right back," was the reply.

Soon he was traveling full speed back to the Ramsey Island bank. He waved as he went by.

He hadn't been gone ten minutes until we came to the bank. Our lines showed that all the leads were bouncing on the bottom at thirty-five fathoms depth. Fifteen minutes later we were in heavy fishing! We did not have a radio telephone and couldn't tell the other boat to come back. However, when he left, the skipper told all the fishermen in Hecate Straits by radio that there were no fish on the Horse Shoe bank, so we were left there alone for three more days of banner fishing! Not until the fourth day did the fleet move in. Fishing had slacked to nothing on the Ramsey Island bank. Knowing that I had not returned, they concluded I was in fish again, so the entire fleet had come.

It was a matter of about five or six hours of good fishing until that bank was fished out. But we had a very good catch—over twelve thousand pounds of number-one kings. On this one trip, I caught more salmon than my father caught that entire summer season! But I also learned the important lesson of obedience to God's leading and was given less and less to doubting Him.

10

HOW TO FIND THE WILL OF GOD

But my days of seminary didn't go as smoothly as they did on the fishing banks.

My first two weeks at the seminary passed without conflict, but I sensed a contrast to the classroom atmosphere of the Bible school from which I had freshly graduated. In the Bible school the Christian faith was dynamic, something you lived and were involved with. The Word of God was taught in an existential life-related way. We reacted to and followed the teaching of Christ's Word.

But at seminary, Christian faith was theoretical and philosophical. We were told to dissect it and look at it objectively. The professors said, in effect, "Don't be concerned about the sin in your own heart, but rather the characteristics of sin in the world." Nor were we directed to look at our own faith. Rather, "faith" was defined as a characteristic of the Church, remote and "out there" somewhere. Generally speaking, the teaching was not at all personal or life-related. The Scriptures were no longer considered *primary evidence*. We were not encouraged to seek "what the Bible teaches." Instead, "what the theologians say the Bible teaches."

Before long, I realized I was fighting for my faith. All manner of spiritual doubts assailed me—primarily in the assigned reading that we were given. From my church, my pastor, and Bible school teachers, I had learned to love the Scriptures. I trusted them implicitly. I believed the Bible was actually God's revelation to man, that "holy men of God wrote it under the inspiration of the Holy Spirit." On a number of occasions, God had even spoken to me personally in the words of the Bible.

At the seminary, however, we were assigned to read books by theologians who not only questioned my faith, but who seemed bent on destroying that faith! They subtilely attacked the authority and the inspiration of the Bible. Having been an agnostic myself, I was converted by the Holy Spirit through the living words of the Bible. I found it difficult to believe any other converted thinking man would not have the same beliefs. Yet we were assigned to read the works of "theologians" who were "demythologizing" the Bible by explaining away any supernatural interventions of God in the Bible as mere "myths to illustrate a deeper truth."

But I *knew from experience* that the Lord intervenes in the lives of humans. He had intervened in mine and brought about my conversion. He had revived my son from sure death. God had worked through me in my service in our church. Even in my fishing ventures, He had worked miracles. There was absolutely no question in my mind that He had also intervened in the lives of all those mentioned in the Bible.

Midway into my second year at the seminary, I went through a "valley" experience, spiritually. Doubt and unbelief constantly assailed me. I became depressed and confused. I even questioned my salvation and the forgiveness of my sins. Guilt confounded my problems. I wondered if the continued bombardment of my faith had taken its toll. It seemed God had left me. My prayers seemed to be empty cliches.

One night as I sat in my study at home thinking out loud, the idea returned to give up the whole idea of the ministry and go back to Seattle.

"If I can't take care of my own soul's needs, how dare I think I can take care of others?" I reasoned.

In this state of mind, I began to pray: "Lord, I am confused. I don't know where I stand with You anymore. I have been fighting for the faith that I once had, but it seems gone with the wind. Lord, speak to me and lift me out of this doubt and depression, or I'll have to quit seminary and forget about becoming a preacher. I have my Bible here. I still believe it's Your Word. Please, speak to me in some way. Unless You come to my rescue, I'll have to give up."

I opened my Bible and began to read. I kept reading and became aware of God's presence in what I read. I became refreshed at the lives of faith and commitment demonstrated by the Apostles. In my study for nearly five hours, I read book after book.

Suddenly, I felt a growing awareness of the presence of God.

The fears and doubts which had been building up in my soul were broken down. I could see no one, but *knew* that Someone was in the room with me. My eyes, blurred from fatigue and depression, tried to focus on the page. Then words leaped up from the Bible and burned into my consciousness. "My grace is sufficient for thee . . . "

Instantly there was recognition in my thought processes. Like a spark gapping across electrical connections, I was aware that God was speaking to me! There was no voice in the room, but my mind "heard" Him speak.

"Herb, you have struggled hard to believe. You know that I exist because of the ways I have made Myself known to you. It doesn't matter what others say. You *know* Me. So trust Me. Believe and obey Me. Have confidence in My resources. Remember, My grace is sufficient for you!"

The room seemed to be spinning and alive with the electricity of His presence. Like a child in the dark reassured by his father, I was overwhelmed with a sense of peace and assurance. Doubts melted away. Fears gave way as I spontaneously began to thank and praise God.

From that day on I kept my rendezvous with the Lord daily. It was as though I had been freshly converted. The joy of the experience overwhelmed me. As I looked to Jesus through His Word, I learned a very important lesson. I learned how to feed my soul even in the wilderness, something that helped me greatly in years that followed.

During my last year of seminary training, I became burdened for the Northwest. As a former deacon in Seattle, I knew there was an "impossible" task to be done to reach people in that area. Only twenty percent of the people there went to church, compared to much higher percentages in the Midwest. "Feelers" came my way from Midwestern churches, but I was very emphatic in saying that I felt called to the West Coast. However, months rolled along and no call came. Most of my classmates had received their calls. Then a written letter of call did come—but not from the West Coast. It came from the Board of Deacons of the Nazareth English Lutheran Church in Minneapolis where I had served as an interim co-pastor.

I took this invitation before the Lord in prayer. My thought was not to accept it.

"Lord," I prayed, "I believe You have given me this burden for the West Coast. That's why I can't believe You would have me accept the call to this Minneapolis church. But this is the only call that has come. Do You want me there? You know I want Your will to be done above everything else."

As I prayed, I wrestled within myself. Was I being honest with the Lord? *Did I really want His will above everything else?* I recalled reading George Mueller's essay on "Finding the Will of God." He wrote, "Ninety percent of the battle in seeking the will of the Lord is not to have a will of your own."

"Lord, how do I divest myself of my own will? I have committed myself to do Your will. But perhaps that was mere form and ritual. So, again, right now, I give up my will. I have been second-guessing Your will. I have chosen the West Coast because that is what *I* want. But is it what You want? Lord, if You want me to accept this call to the Nazareth Church, that is exactly what I want to do."

I continued in prayerful meditation, waiting for the still small voice of God. The Spirit of God within me vividly impressed this thought on my consciousness: "Accept this call. I have a purpose and ministry for you there. After your training there, I will call you out of Nazareth even as I called Christ out of Nazareth."

"Thank you, Lord, for this inner guidance," I responded. "I

will write a letter of acceptance." There was immediate joy and peace in my decision.

With the call from a congregation comes the right to ordination. I was ordained in my home church in Seattle following graduation from seminary. It was a meaningful, joyous day for me as I was set apart for God's ministry.

I returned to Minneapolis and was installed as the pastor of the Nazareth Church. I began working immediately through home visits to share Christ, counsel people and invite them to our church services. Soon, our little church grew to more than one hundred in regular attendance. Likewise our Sunday School was growing as we reached young people through ministry in the Word.

Then one day a few months later I received a letter. It was a call from the Central Lutheran Church in Anchorage, Alaska.

"This call is premature," I thought. "I can't leave after such a short term of office, especially since we're experiencing such growth and revival."

I called on my friend, Dr. Oscar Hanson, president of Lutheran Bible Institute. I told him of the letter and my own thinking. He nodded in agreement.

"Mjorud, you'll receive many calls like this one. It's impossible for you to leave your present parish, serving there such a short time. Send back your regrets."

I thanked him for his advice, convinced he was right. I would turn back the call.

However, a few days later, I met Dr. Philip Dybvig, director of home missions in our church body. I casually mentioned to him my call to Anchorage.

"Pastor Mjorud, there is no one trained like you are for that call. You've been a fisherman. You've lived in Alaska. You know the hearts of the people on the West Coast. I believe that call is tailor made for you."

During the next few weeks, I sought advice from many others. The more advice I received, the more confused I became. I knew I had to come to grips with this call with the Lord alone. I could not rely on human guidance—it was contradictory and confusing. I had to have God's guidance once again.

One evening, I told Gundhild, "I'm going into my office and don't want to be disturbed. I'm not coming out until I know what the Lord wants me to do with the Anchorage call."

In my study I listed the "pros" and "cons" in respect to that call. Soon, I had full columns of reasons beneath each heading.

"Look at this, Lord," I prayed. "I can easily accept or reject this call and justify my decision. But I have not come to do my will nor justify *my* actions. I come for Your guidance, Your answer in respect to what I am to do with this call."

Then I did something I'd never done before. I wrote a prayer to the Lord. I explained my fear of serving Him by going my own way, doing my own thing. I knew that I was adept at doing things in my own strength and wisdom and told the Lord. I recalled Scriptures where I was called to "deny myself, take up my cross and follow Him." Midway into that prayer, I recalled something that Samuel had said to Saul: "Then the Spirit of the Lord shall come upon you mightily, and you shall prophesy with them and be changed into another man . . . then do what seems right to you under the circumstances for the Spirit of God is with you" (I Samuel 10:6,7).

In my written prayer, I thanked God He had sent the Spirit of God to me to make me a new man in Christ. In light of this, what was God's will now that I had become a son of God? Then I weighed the call from Anchorage. The Lord knew I had been burdened for the Northwest. My heart was with *those* people. The answer was clear. Laborers were plentiful in Minneapolis, but few in Anchorage. I knew it was right for me to go.

I found myself writing, "Lord, I believe it is right for me to go to Anchorage. I believe this call is from You. So unless You close the door, I'll accept this call and go to Anchorage."

The peace of God flooded my soul, and I once again had the inner confirmation that I was doing the will of God.

It was after midnight when I came out of my office to the living room. Gundhild was still there.

"I have the Lord's answer. We're going to Anchorage."

She smiled. "I've known that all along, even from the day that the letter came."

In facing this decision I became conscious of a growing dependence upon the leading of God and the guidance of the Holy Spirit. Discovering God's will was not difficult or mysterious. Using the Bible as my resource, I learned principles of decision making. God puts each of us into different backgrounds and situations. It seems reasonable and practical that He use our training, learning and experiences to best advantage. As I read in I Samuel 10, we do what is best under the circumstances. Since we are "new creatures in Christ," eager to do His will and purpose, our thinking is guided by the spiritual principles we learn as believers.

The factor which makes all this practical is looking to the way God has guided and led in the past. He brings a variety of joys and gains into our life experiences. These shape our character and talents. We must ask ourselves, "Because of these experiences, what can I do better than anyone else? And, what is it I am now doing that someone else can do as well or better?" Thus if we know of a need that someone else can fill, then we should look elsewhere. God often wants us to fill a need no one could meet as well.

I tried to remember these principles of guidance and to apply them to everyday decision making. I believe it gave a spiritual dimension to every choice I made, since every one I made was done by taking God's purposes into consideration.

It was a spiritual exercise God used to prepare me for my next exciting lesson in faith and trust.

11

ANOINTING OF THE HOLY SPIRIT

"It's a slow go to reach souls for Christ here in Anchorage," the Reverend Robert Palmer, pastor of Spenard Chapel, greeted me on my arrival. "Only God can break through. We have started a pastors' prayer meeting to share our burdens. Would you be interested?"

"I'll be there!" I assured him. The next Thursday morning I met with them.

I found these pastors who attended this prayer meeting were of one heart and mind. We were all born of the same Spirit, were called, and were serving the same Lord. We shared a common burden, although we represented different denominations. We prayed for our city leaders, the churches of Anchorage, the pastors, for each other, and for the particular concerns of each man present.

I prayed for God's power in preaching the Word. I did this during my personal prayer time and while with the pastors on Thursday mornings. But something seemed wrong. Things were not happening. Spiritual results which had come so easily in Minneapolis were not taking place here.

One Sunday morning, a year after my arrival in that parish, I was in my study praying before the morning worship service.

"O Lord," I began, "I believe that these words in my sermon are Your words. I know You want these people saved. I also know that conversion is the work of the Holy Spirit. So, Lord, I want to get out of Your way. Use me, but only in Your power. Give me a heart compassion for these people. Let nothing of my own ego and mind get in the way. Let my words come forth under the power of the Holy Spirit. I ask this in Jesus' name."

I opened my eyes. They fell upon a verse in my open Bible on my desk: *Whatever you ask in prayer, believe that you receive, and you will* (Mark 11:24).

God, in specific answer to my prayer, appeared to be assuring me I could have the power of the Holy Spirit working for and through me. All I had to do was ask for it, believe I'd receive it, and I would!

Really? Was it that simple?

"O Lord," I said. "I know I am Your child, born of Your Spirit. I know You have called me to this congregation to preach Your Word to them. I believe it is Your will that I preach in the power of the Holy Spirit. I ask You now specifically for that power. I believe now I have that power. Thank you, Lord Jesus, for anointing me with the Holy Spirit, Amen."

There were no lightning flashes in the heavens, no particular feelings or sensations, just an inner heart conviction that I was the Lord's servant and that His power was now with me.

I had been more or less an apologist for the faith, perhaps because of my legal training. I preached as a defender of the faith. Now the Lord inwardly impressed upon me, "You do not have to defend Me or the faith. I have called you to proclaim the faith."

From that point, I saw men in a new light. I saw them through the eyes of love and not judgment. Suddenly I was excited and eager to communicate this Gospel of love. I walked out to the sanctuary and looked at the people sitting there. I sensed a new compassion for them. When I preached the sermon that morning, there was a calm sense of urgency. There was a new liberty, even from my notes.

As I preached, I sensed a special intuition that my message was truly a word from the Lord. Although there was nothing tangible to notice after that service, I knew in my heart we would have a harvest.

Several weeks later, a woman came to my office. She was a contractor's wife and a member of the church. Before I could seat her, she said, "Pastor, I can't stand your preaching! Either I have to get right with God or leave this church. I can't sleep at night. I'm a nervous wreck!"

In my heart I said, "Well, praise the Lord!" Outwardly I said, "Please have a seat. I am sure I can help you."

Slowly and deliberately she unfolded her double life. "I am sick and tired of going to dances, cocktail parties, and living the kind of life I lead. It was all right until I began to attend church. I pretend to be a Christian. I am the worst kind of a hypocrite. I *know* I'm wrong—that I'm what the Bible calls a sinner! I know I am not right with God and I want to make a new start. Can you help me?"

"Yes, I can," I said calmly. "It's obvious the Holy Spirit has been working in your life. He has made you take an honest look at yourself. He has convicted you of your sin and unbelief, not to punish or torture you—but to get your attention focused on your need. You now know you need Jesus Christ."

She began to weep. I told her how she could be totally forgiven and have a new life in and through Jesus Christ.

Then we prayed. She poured out her heart before the Lord, mincing no words about her life of sin, compromise and pretense. As she prayed, her sobs of anguish turned to obvious joy even though the tears were still streaming. She was repeating, "Thank You, Lord, thank You."

She regained her composure, smiled, stood up and thanked me. "Now I can stay in this church with peace of mind."

Two weeks later we had an evangelist at our church for five days of meetings. During the evening service, I was making some announcements, when this woman who had come to Christ two weeks earlier stood up and said, "May I say something?"

I gave her my consent, and she faced the congregation.

"I have to ask you as a congregation to forgive me," she began slowly. "I have been singing in the choir, teaching

Sunday School, but living a double life. Most of you already know this. I had one foot in the church, but the other in the world. I lived a compromising, hypocritical life. But I want you to know that I've been forgiven by the Lord. Now, I know Him in a new way that has given me joy, peace and a brand new outlook."

Her words were electrifying to people who were living the same way as she had before her conversion. The evangelist preached his sermon, pointing out that "many decent respectable church-going people need to be converted," and dealing primarily with the sin of unbelief and the rejection of Christ. After the sermon he gave an invitation. That evening twenty-six people confessed their sins and opened their hearts to receive Jesus Christ as Savior! Revival began at Central Lutheran Church in the "last frontier."

From that point everything changed. I dealt with troubled souls who were full of repentance and were ready to accept Jesus Christ as Savior. Some came to my office, others stayed after services, some called and asked me to come to their homes. More than once the phone rang and someone, weeping on the other end, cried out, "I am one of those decent respectable church-going people who is not converted. Can you come out and help me?"

Another woman, married to the "town drunk," asked me to place her husband on my prayer list. After a few months, he came to my office one day.

"I came home a few weeks ago and found my wife and son on their knees. My son was praying for me to be converted from alcoholism. I had a flask of whiskey on my hip, and those words of my son broke my heart, so I went into the kitchen, took the whiskey and emptied it in the sink, vowing to never drink again. But that lasted only a week. Here I am, hooked by drinking again. Can you help me?"

12

PRAYER OF FAITH HEALS THE SICK

Anchorage had more alcoholics per capita than any United States city except Washington, D.C. I believed the problem of the alcoholic was a spiritual one, a matter of sin, guilt and bondage. An alcoholic needed forgiveness, but he also needed deliverance. And this deliverance was a kind of *healing.* Jesus Christ was the answer, for in Him there was forgiveness *and* deliverance.

We dealt with alcoholics on this basis and discovered that the Lord could really rescue them from drink. It wasn't long before our church was more successful in dealing with alcoholics than Alcoholics Anonymous!

In dealing with alcoholics, I counseled with them until they knew and admitted their bondage to alcohol. Then it was a matter of claiming not only forgiveness through Jesus Christ, but deliverance based on the power of the Holy Spirit. Healing of their bodies from the tyranny of alcoholism resulted when these men and women called upon God for this power. Soon we had a dozen or so men and some women who were completely delivered and healed of alcoholism. I regarded their deliverance as miraculous and often spoke of it as a miracle.

If I had been logical in my faith at that time, I'd have realized it was no greater difficulty for the power of God to heal other sicknesses as easily as alcoholism. That logical deduction somehow escaped my mind, conditioned as we all are to natural explanations and boundaries.

I had many opportunities to pray for the sick as a parish pastor. Hospital calling was a part of my weekly routine. I visited the Anchorage General Hospital as well as hospitals for Elmendorf Air Force Base and Fort Richardson Army Base. There were many sick to call upon every week. My counsel and prayers were primarily concerned with their relationship with Jesus Christ as Savior, not Healer. But I was familiar with the words of Jesus Christ, "In my name you shall lay your hands upon the sick and they shall recover." Those words often came to mind when I saw someone seriously ill or injured. I also was moved at times by an inner urge and compassion to lay hands upon these sick in accordance with the Lord's words. However, there was no courage or faith in me during those days to do so.

I had been taught theologically that any prayer for God's intervention to heal had to be prefaced with, "Lord, if it be Thy will," not realizing this made the prayer one of *doubt* instead of *faith*. Hence, my prayers brought no supernatural intervention to sick bodies. Some people were healed, but through natural healing processes, medicine, or professional care.

There were, however, several exceptions that confused and unnerved me. One day Major George Gould came to my office. Without giving time for the usual exchange of niceties, he came bluntly to the point of his visit.

"I know I am not right with God. I need salvation like my wife has recently received. And I need healing. I have a pinched nerve in my neck that gives me a chronic stiff neck. I want you to lay hands on me for the healing of my neck."

I had met Major Gould before. He, his wife, and two children had become regular attenders at our church services and I had led his wife to a personal commitment to Jesus Christ. She was converted and found peace with God. Her husband had seen what a difference Christ had made in her life, and was now asking for the same thing himself.

I counseled with Major Gould and asked him to pray, confess his sins, and open his heart to Jesus Christ. After a tearful, repentant confession, I heard him pray, "Thank You,

Lord, for saving my soul."

After a few moments, he turned to me.

"Okay, Pastor, now lay hands upon me so I will be healed."

I was startled, but on the other hand marvelled at this man's faith. What could I say? His request was Scriptural. I trusted God and did what he requested.

"I lay hands upon you in Jesus' name for healing." But before I could add, "Lord, if it be Thy will," Major Gould was excitedly praising the Lord again.

"Thank You, Lord! You've healed me!"

He began to move and twist his head, testing for the painful pinched nerve.

"It's gone, Pastor! It's all gone. The Lord *did* heal me!"

I was dumbfounded, both by the miracle and the complete trusting faith of this man. He was "naive enough" to believe. He didn't "know better." I hid my own unbelief and behaved as though this kind of experience happened every day. This incident had a profound subconscious effect on me. But consciously I had the same reservations toward healing as before.

However, a year later I was called to the home of Mr. and Mrs. Alvin Moe, devoted members of our congregation. Their baby boy was in the hospital suffering from double pneumonia. An excessive accumulation of fluids had collapsed one lung. The baby's condition was critical. Gundhild and I entered the Moe home. Mrs. Moe was bravely speaking to us about their baby's condition, smiling through her tears. We knelt to pray in their living room. My wife and his wife prayed. Alvin prayed.

Then it was my turn to pray. As I concluded my prayer, Alvin stood up and said, "The Lord is healing my son! I don't know how, but I believe the baby is being healed."

Alvin disappeared and soon reappeared again. He had changed into his working clothes as a cement finisher and soon excused himself.

"I feel at peace now. Everything is under control. I am going back to work," he said.

I admired his faith, but wondered if it wasn't just wishful thinking.

Amazingly, we learned from the hospital the baby had begun to improve at that very moment! But, as a test of faith, his collapsed lung did not inflate as expected. Doctors said that if it did not inflate within two weeks, surgery would be necessary to remove that lung. We were told that it was impossible for a lung collapsed more than two weeks to regain its usefulness. Three weeks went by and the lung still did not inflate, so surgery was planned. But surgeons could not operate until the baby's body was built up to full stamina. Five weeks went by before the doctors agreed they could perform surgery.

On the day the boy was to have his surgery, at the mother's insistence, doctors took another X-ray. To their astonishment the pictures showed the lung was perfectly normal.

"Never in known medical history has a lung inflated after two weeks!" one doctor said.

Other medical experts agreed. All were amazed.

"We have seen a miracle," observed another doctor.

I was both impressed and confused by what I had encountered. The Lord was again planting a new seed of faith and growth within my own heart. A miracle? But certainly not because of *my* faith. I had doubts and little faith. *Yet strong, deep faith was present in both healings.* I "filed" that experience away, still uncertain how to deal with the subject of God's healing.

One afternoon a member of my congregation, George Risvold, telephoned. He sounded urgent.

"Pastor, can you come right over? I'm in deep trouble."

George was city assessor, a man in his fifties, married to Mildred, a school teacher. Both were devoted members of our congregation. George was obviously very ill.

Weakly he turned to me and said, "I've been to the local clinic and had a thorough physical examination. The aorta valve of my heart isn't working. The nerves are dying. When my heart beats, the valve in the aorta doesn't close all the way. So I've got bad blood circulation and poisons are building up in my body. The doctors told me they don't know any cure for this condition. They say there's nothing they can do." He blinked back tears.

"Pastor," George concluded, "I'm dying. I've only got a couple months, unless God helps me. But, Pastor, what's James 5:14 in the Bible for?"

I opened my Bible, but George recited it, "*If anyone is sick, let him call the elders of the church and anoint him with oil.*"

Then he added, "Mildred and I have been looking at that verse real hard."

"Well, I guess it's a verse for those who have faith," I offered hesitantly.

"I have faith!" George shot right back. "I believe that that verse is true for us today."

I was walking on thin ice. Slowly I asked the obvious, "What do you want me to do?"

"Let's do what the Bible says," he said with confidence. "Call the deacons and have them pray over me and anoint me with oil."

"Very well," I said. "How about two o'clock tomorrow afternoon?" The following day was Saturday and the deacons would not be working. "I'll call the deacons and we'll meet you at church."

"That's fine with me," he answered. "I'll get someone to help me get there."

We chatted awhile longer, then prayed together, asking the Lord to guide in this situation. Driving home, I wondered about the service—laying on of hands and anointing with oil. How was it done? What should I do?

Upon returning to my office, I began to search my library to find something about how to conduct a healing service. I couldn't find anything on the subject. Even in commentaries amplifying the background and meaning of the fifth chapter of James there was nothing which told of procedures for a healing service.

"*I'll have to play it by ear,* I concluded. Then I recalled that olive oil must have been used in those days, so I went to a nearby drugstore. I bought a medium-sized bottle of olive oil, hoping the clerk wouldn't ask what I intended to use it for!

When I returned to my study, I remembered something about oil in the consecration of Aaron as High Priest in the Old

81

Testament. I looked up the verse which triggered my memory. It was Psalm 133:2: "It is like the precious oil upon the head, running down upon the beard, upon the beard of Aaron, running down on the collar of his robes."

They must have been generous with the oil, I mused.

Then I began calling the deacons. All six said they'd come to the healing service. I called others whom I knew to be praying Christians and invited them to be present, too.

As I read and reread that fifth chapter of James, one phrase caught my attention: *"The prayer of faith will heal the sick."*

Maybe, I was thinking, *if I call enough Christians, someone among us might be able to pray that prayer of faith.*

There were fourteen of us, including George and Mildred, when we came together for the healing service. I explained why we were meeting, and related something of George's ailment, and how we would proceed. I read James 5:14 and 15: "Is any among you sick? Let him call for the elders of the church, and let them pray over him, anointing him with oil in the name of the Lord; and the prayer of faith will save the sick man, and the Lord will raise him up; and if he has committed sins, he will be forgiven."

I asked them all to kneel at the altar and pray, one after the other, until all had prayed. Then I called the deacons to stand with me around George as I anointed him with oil.

I reread the same verses and said, "Lord, *we are claiming this promise* for our brother George Risvold. I anoint him with oil in the name of the Father (whereupon I poured oil upon George's head) and the Son (and I poured more oil upon his head) and the Holy Spirit (and I poured still more oil on his head). We do this in the holy name of Jesus Christ, our Savior and Lord, Amen."

The oil was running down George's hair, over his face, and down his neck. I asked the deacons to lay their hands upon George's head, together with me. Again we all prayed, holding to the words which I had read in James, chapter five.

As soon as we took our hands off George, he stood up. I didn't have the courage to ask him, "Do you feel better, George?" I didn't have to.

"Well, I feel much better," he said simply.

The service was over. Everyone quietly moved out of the church—as though we had been to a funeral service, for we Lutherans are wont to be solemn, especially during rites and special services.

I watched George walk out without any help. When he had come in, he had been supported by his friend on one side, and Mildred on the other side. Yet I was still afraid to believe we had helped him.

But George was miraculously healed! He took a plane the next day to Toronto, Canada, and had heart specialists there examine him thoroughly. They found his heart to be perfect. He came back to Anchorage two weeks later and went through the same clinic for examinations. To the astonishment of his doctors, they discovered his heart had been totally healed!

My skeptical mind wanted to know more.

George told us later, "When I was anointed with oil in the name of Jesus and the deacons put their hands on my head and prayed, it felt like electricity going down from head through my body! All that power seemed focused on my heart. I could feel something happening inside me, as though my heart was being knit together. I *knew* I was being instantly healed by the Lord. But before I could tell anyone publicly about this healing, I wanted medical verification. And you know what both teams of heart specialists report. All the doctors found my heart to be perfect!"

George is very much alive at this writing, some eighteen years later, having retired from an active life, and is living with his wife in Arlington, Washington.

I marvelled at this wonderful miracle of healing. I had to say to myself, "The Word of God really works when there is faith. I wonder who prayed the prayer of faith in that healing service for George. I'm sure it wasn't me. Surely the faith of George, which held on to that promise in James, was an active ingredient. But George's faith is not my faith."

Despite these three events, I still didn't suggest healing services for anyone else. I was still reluctant to believe all that the Word of God said about healing. What I didn't realize was that God was opening my mind to a wider acceptance of His power and Being.

13

WHERE DID THE REVIVAL GO?

Dr. Maynard Force, president of the Lutheran Bible Institute of Los Angeles, served as teacher for a week of camp near Anchorage. The meetings were great—and so was the response to God's Word.

One afternoon during that week, Dr. Force and I were chatting. Our conversation turned to the subject of revival for our Lutheran churches in America. We discovered we both were concerned about the need for evangelism and spiritual growth. We ended our time together on our knees. Then we agreed to meet each day for further prayer.

On Saturday, the last afternoon of camp and the last time we'd have together, my eyes fell upon my open Bible on the chair before me. These words stood out as though they were italicized: *Behold you shall call nations that you know not and nations that knew you not shall run to you because of the Lord your God and of the holy one of Israel, for He has glorified you* (Isaiah 55:5).

I had a deep sense of understanding that the Holy Spirit meant those words for me. Yet I was bewildered. What did they mean?

I was so caught up in this puzzle that Dr. Force had to ask me, "Herb, what's the matter?"

All I could manage was, "Dr. Force, I believe God has

spoken to me . . . but I'm not sure of the meaning. I'm afraid I can't tell you just now what it is. Perhaps later."

When I was alone, I took another long look at those words: "You shall call nations—nations shall run to you—I have glorified you."

How could these words apply to me? Reading the words over again, I readily recalled how they had virtually leaped off the page that afternoon. Was I being presumptuous? No, I was not looking for such a verse to massage my ego. I wasn't even certain of the meaning. I had no plans for missionary service overseas.

Later that evening, I tried to share the incident with Gundhild. "I just don't understand why the Spirit gave me this promise. It seems too mysterious, so unrealistic."

Gundhild agreed. "Don't let it trouble you, though. God will show you the meaning in His own time . . . . But it does seem rather 'far out.' "

When we returned to Anchorage after the Bible camp, two letters were waiting. One was from the headquarters of our church body. It was an official call to become an evangelist for the Evangelical Lutheran Church (now merged into the American Lutheran Church). The other letter was from the director of evangelism. His was a personal plea for me to prayerfully consider this call. He expressed his concern for revival.

I had received this call twice before but had turned it down with the excuse, "We're in the midst of revival and I can't leave now."

My first reaction was to refuse this call for the same reason. Our congregation, I thought, needed me to keep going. Or did they? I remembered my call from Minneapolis. The Lord had taken me out of a growing ministry then.

"I'm sorry, Lord," I chuckled. "I'd forgotten that I'm not indispensable. You can remove me and find someone else easily."

So I made the letter a matter of prayer. As I did, I was overwhelmed with a heavy burden for revival in churches everywhere. Then came the Lord's answer.

"This call is for you. Accept it."

The next Sunday I let the congregation know the Lord had called me into a new work. There were different reactions to my decision. Some said, "We knew you'd be leaving soon and we know this is God's will."

Others shook their heads and said, "Pastor, your decision is insane!"

I smiled. They both were right. So we moved back to Minneapolis which appeared geographically central to traveling across the country to different churches.

Everywhere I went in the months that followed, I found an openness to the message of repentance and salvation. In some places there was great responsiveness. I encouraged people not right with God to make a decision of faith. Altar calls were not traditional in our Lutheran churches, so I encouraged people to make this decision in silent prayer in the pew. In some services after silent prayer, I persuaded people to make a decision of faith to God by raising their hand to Jesus Christ to indicate that decision. I always encouraged people to stay after the service for counsel, if they had not already received the help they were seeking.

I knew that "decisions for Christ" would not always be well received. Some pastors and church officials let me know they were not in favor of such interruptions in traditional Lutheran church decorum. However, I continued the practice wherever I went, in spite of their opposition. The results following the services, and later letters of testimony telling of changed lives following these decisions, confirmed the rightness of the action.

In one Lutheran church in Washington, my sermon was basically a testimony of my conversion experience. There was time for silent prayer of decision. But as we were singing the closing hymn, I invited anyone who desired to come forward to the altar to do so. No one came. Then as we sang the last stanza a woman walked down the aisle to the altar. I suggested we sing the first stanza again. During the singing of this verse, people came forward in such numbers there were only a few left in the pews!

I counseled them on repentance, forgiveness of sins, and salvation through Jesus Christ. I then asked them to pray, confessing their sins. There were tears of confession from the entire crowd, climaxed by tears of joy as they invited Jesus Christ into their hearts and lives. What a transformation came to them as a congregation, according to a letter the pastor wrote me several weeks later.

The Lord demonstrated His presence in summer Bible camps for young people as well as in churches.

I taught in the mornings and preached every evening. The messages were on the sins of youth and the need for repentance and salvation through Jesus Christ.

One of the pastors complained.

"Mjorud, you're treating our young people as though they are heathen! Why don't you go easy on that hellfire and brimstone."

At one camp that first year I went to the faculty cabin to retire after the evening meeting. But shortly after I got there, a girls' counselor knocked on my door.

"You will have to come to my cabin. I just can't quiet the girls!" she said.

As we came near the cabin, I could hear that girls were crying. When we walked in the door, they burst into convulsive sobbing.

"I know what has happened to all of you," I told them. "The same thing happened to me many years ago when I opened my heart to Jesus Christ. Let me read something to you from the Bible."

I turned the pages of my Bible and began to read from Ezekiel 36:26: "A new heart I will give you, and a new spirit I will put within you; and I will take out of your flesh the heart of stone and give you a heart of flesh."

The weeping subsided, and I said, "Now, isn't this the same thing God did for you tonight?"

"Why yes," said one of the girls, smiling through red and swollen eyes. "The Lord has given all of us a new heart. I was the first to come back to our cabin and I knelt and cried when I came in. Then two others came in and asked me, 'Did it happen to you, too?' and when I said, 'Yes,' they joined me and were crying too. Then three others came, and the same thing happened all over again, and right behind them, the rest of them. We learned that all of us had the same experience during that service. It's really great."

"Yes," explained another. "We're not crying because we're upset. It's because we're so happy and feel good."

However, there were adversaries. At the Bible camp where God's love and power changed the lives of fifty-seven out of a group of one hundred of these young people, there was intense opposition by the pastors.

Many of the ministers in the Lutheran churches were against decisions of faith, saying my ministry was Baptist instead of Lutheran. Conversion experiences and weeping were "nothing but emotionalism." They had been taught to believe that Christian faith begins with early baptism, to be nurtured through lifelong teaching, preaching, and the Lord's Supper. When they heard people testify of conversion, peace with God, and changed lives, they were confused. Not understanding such experiences, they were against my ministry. Though I found this kind of opposition from many pastors and leaders in Lutheran churches, there were some who were with me. I was grateful for their cooperation.

But from my own conversion experience, the revivals I witnessed in my two churches and in congregations open to my evangelistic ministry, I believed I had some answers. Spiritual awakening—with both salvation and renewal—were supernatural occurrences. I was committed to do everything humanly possible to bring each of them about. An inner peace assured me that I was on the right track.

Statistics from the evangelism office showed only ten percent of Evangelical Lutheran Churches ever had an evangelist visit. Most of the churches were closed to evangelists.

I knew there had to be a more effective and faster way, if we were to see the entire church body revived. I regarded the Lutheran Church generally as a sleeping giant. If it could only

89

be revived, it could quickly bring the Gospel to the entire world!

But there was another problem. I was disconcerted to see spiritual interest flare during a crusade but then die out in the months that followed.

In one congregation, for example, many testified to finding Christ as their personal Savior during the week of evangelism. Attendance increased every night. The final services were packed out. The prayer meeting preceding the services increased from a handful to a hundred. The enthusiasm for the Kingdom of God was exciting and wonderful. But I returned one year later, and it appeared as though nothing had ever happened! Everything had to be started all over again.

I recall asking, "Where did the revival go? What is wrong, Lord? How quickly they fall back into ineffective activity. Is there a missing link?"

14

EDIFYING MYSELF

I believed what the Bible said concerning the Holy Spirit. And after all, I reasoned, "Didn't I receive an anointing of the Holy Spirit myself in Anchorage that Sunday when I claimed His power in order to preach more effectively? Surely I have been baptized with the Holy Spirit. Isn't this what God promised in Acts 1:8?"

Something bothered me, however. At this time I began to read about a spiritual revival taking place in many historic denominational churches. Pastors and laymen were giving testimony to an experience similar to that of the apostles in the upper room on the day of Pentecost. They told of "speaking in other tongues" as thy worshiped the Lord.

I had no reason to doubt their testimony, but knew there was something here I did not understand. Undoubtedly, I would have received this gift myself if I had sought it. But I felt I did not need it.

However, as I began to hear and read more about this movement of the Holy Spirit, it appeared that where men and women worshiped the Lord in this way He worked miracles. This caused me to study the Bible very carefully. Looking back, I see that I interpreted everything to fit my own doctrine and experiences. I claimed to be openminded. I even said to those around me who called such gifts divisive, "I am sure healing and miracles can be a help in the ministry of the Church. There *is* something to these experiences."

But this really was not my concern. My consuming question was, "How can we revive the Church? How can we build it into a healthy thriving community where all members know forgiveness of sins, are born of the Spirit, and live and walk the victorious life of Jesus Christ?"

Then early in 1962, a retreat was held in St. Paul for the thirteen evangelists of the American Lutheran Church. Only eight of us were present. On the last day, our director gave a report of charismatic involvements he had witnessed on a recent trip.

"I heard testimonies from a number of denominational pastors. They claimed to have had a new experience which they call 'the baptism with the Holy Spirit.' This experience brought healing and miracles into their congregations."

It was apparent our director believed these testimonies implicitly.

"There's a stirring amid the mulberry bushes. Everywhere God is pouring out His Holy Spirit. These reports are coming from across the United States and all over the world. I want you men to keep your hearts and minds open to all that the Holy Spirit is doing. We do not want to be behind the door when God is pouring out His Holy Spirit," he said.

I was fascinated by the report and resolved to take my director's advice.

One of my next calls for a week of evangelism was from a church in Seattle, Washington. I had heard many reports concerning Father Dennis Bennett of St. Luke's Episcopal Church who also was there. Stories were told of reputed healings and miracles in the church. I also had heard of their phenomenal growth. I thought this would be a good opportunity to see firsthand what was happening. So I called Pastor Bennett on the telephone.

"My name is Herbert Mjorud. I'm an evangelist with the Lutheran Church. I'd like to talk with you," I said.

"We have a service here every Friday evening where I explain

'What the Holy Spirit is doing at St. Luke's Church.' Come along if you wish."

"Well, I do have Friday night free. I may see you there," I said, not wanting to commit myself definitely.

"Praise the Lord," he said as he hung up.

Later, I spoke to the pastor of a local Lutheran congregation where I was holding meetings. I asked him what he knew about St. Luke's Church and Father Bennett.

"Oh, they're having a lot of excitement over there, all right." He grinned. "It's become a real pentecostal church. At least one hundred and fifty of their members speak in tongues and go through all kinds of 'Hallelujah' times."

I gathered from his attitude that he wasn't accepting their experiences as orthodox. When he said one hundred and fifty members were speaking in tongues, I imagined all kinds of emotional extremes, wild body contortions—maybe even "holy rolling" on the floor, as I'd been told some pentecostals did. My doctrinal and intellectual guard was up. I even felt nervous and a bit fearful of attending that meeting. I decided to make it a matter of prayer.

"Lord," I prayed, "You always give me an answer when I come to You. I am trusting You to show me the truth of this experience."

Although I had some misgivings and apprehensions, I went to St. Luke's Church that Friday evening.

What a beehive of activity! I sat in back so I could get out in a hurry in case things got out of hand. But I recognized a number of Lutheran people whom I knew quite well. They introduced me to members of St. Luke's.

After several hymns, Father Bennett spoke informally on "What the Holy Spirit is doing at St. Luke's Church." He punctuated his comments with deliberate and precise references to the Bible to support the experiences to which he referred.

I expected a raucous throng, shouting and carrying on in some ecstatic way. But the service was quiet—as orderly as any of my Lutheran services.

Father Bennett told of having many of the same inhibitions

and preconceived ideas that I held before he received the baptism in the Holy Spirit. He told of previously dealing with the rebuking church members for becoming involved in this new "charismatic experience." But then the Lord brought the Holy Spirit and His gifts into his own life—something which led to his resigning his previous church.

"I came to St. Luke's Church at my Bishop's request as kind of an experiment, to see what could happen in a defunct congregation, ready to close its doors. All we do is preach the Word of God, including the message on the Holy Spirit. And as you've seen, our congregation has grown rapidly! The budget has increased three times in two years, and all kinds of miracles happen regularly."

He explained carefully how one might receive the baptism with the Spirit.

"It's for those who already are Christians. It's not only for full-time Christian workers, but the laity as well. The gift of tongues is the evidence of this baptism. It comes with the package. And other gifts of the Spirit follow the gift of speaking in tongues," he said.

I pondered my own experience with the Holy Spirit. I wondered what I was to do now. "Lead me again, Lord," I prayed quietly.

After Pastor Bennett spoke for an hour and forty-five minutes, the meeting ended. There was a short coffeebreak after which there was to be a time of "prayer and praise." I stayed for both.

"During this prayer and praise time, I ask that only our own members take part in evidencing the charismatic gifts so the order to which we are accustomed is maintained," Pastor Bennett said.

One person stood up and spoke in words unknown to me but in a manner no different had the words been spoken in English. Pastor Bennett said, "We have heard a message in tongues; we await the interpretation."

Then someone spoke in English a message he said came from the Lord.

This happened several times. Nothing in the mannerisms of

the participants offended my Lutheran sense of propriety. But now my legal mind needed verification. I was thinking, "Lord You know I need proof to quiet my doubts."

It came almost immediately. The second person who spoke in tongues had spoken in perfect Mandarin Chinese. The one who interpreted gave the sense of that message in English. A Chinese Christian who knew both languages was in the audience and verified the correctness of both!

At this point Pastor Bennett announced, "I must leave now, but we have many ministers trained to help any of you who seek help. How many of our people are here tonight? Raise your hands."

About seventy or eighty raised their hands.

"These are our ministers," he explained. "They will help you whether it be for salvation, healing, deliverance, or the baptism with the Spirit."

What a church! I thought. *Every time people stay after services for counseling in our Lutheran churches, I am the one left to do the work. Here in this relatively young congregation, seventy to eighty workers are ready to help.*

Is this the "missing link" in our own attempts at bringing revival to our Lutheran congregations? I asked myself.

In the sanctuary a young man came up to me and introduced himself. "I'm a member of St. Luke's. I'd like to help if you're seeking the Lord."

I shook his hand. "No, thank you. I'm Herb Mjorud. I'm an evangelist in town this week."

"Are you seeking the baptism with the Spirit?" he asked.

"Well, yes and no," I responded. "I had an experience of being empowered by the Holy Spirit when I was in the parish ministry. I know this was an anointing of the Spirit to preach. Many things your pastor said tonight are new to me, however. I have several questions in my mind now as to whether I really was baptized with the Spirit."

"Do you speak with other tongues?" my friend asked.

"No, I don't."

"Would you like to pray with me?"

"Why sure," I answered. "I'm always ready to pray."

We knelt down next to the last pew.

"Are you seeking the gifts of the Spirit?" he asked.

"Yes, the gifts of wisdom, knowledge and perhaps healing," I answered.

"What about the gift of speaking in other tongues?"

"No, that doesn't fit in with our Lutheran Church," I said.

"Do you know that by what you just said you're not in the will of God?" he queried firmly.

I shifted slightly to control myself from being ruffled. He did not mean it as rudeness. He was earnest.

"How do you mean?" was my response.

"Well, the Bible says we should desire the spiritual gifts. One of those gifts is the gift of speaking in other tongues, which you say you do not want. In effect, you are saying to God, 'I will take this gift but not that one.' You are closing yourself off from gifts because God is not really sovereign in your asking."

"I see the wisdom with which you speak," I said.

I knew very well the Scriptures he referred to and was amazed. I had not seen this truth before.

"Pray with me for *all* gifts, including tongues," I said. "Since it is God's will, I am ready to speak in a thousand tongues."

By now two other young men from the church had joined us. After introductions, we began praying.

I prayed, then my first friend prayed. We asked the Lord to baptize me with the Holy Spirit. He laid his hand upon me and said, "Evangelist Mjorud receive this blessing of the baptism with the Holy Spirit from Jesus Christ who is here present."

And I said, "Yes, Lord, I gladly receive what You now have for me."

Then my friend said, "Thank the Lord now by faith for this blessing. Now you can speak in other tongues!"

I opened my mouth expecting that in some way the Holy Spirit would use my mouth. But not a sound.

"Nothing comes," I said, almost apologetically.

My three friends encouraged me further.

I said, "Lord, I am willing; take hold of my speech faculties and let me speak."

This went on and on. Their exhortations became labored.

One after another they were praying in other tongues and in English. I did not know what to do. They were kind and patient with my apparent failure.

I began to wonder what was wrong with me. People were leaving the church. Apparently, all had received and had spoken in tongues, judging from all the jubilation they exhibited. We were the only ones left.

"Brother Mjorud . . . *claim* the gift of tongues in Jesus' name."

I did. Nothing.

"Sir, do you have misgivings in respect to this gift? Do you hold reservations in your mind against this gift?"

"I'm sure I must. I've been 'brainwashed' against the gift with all kinds of theological presuppositions. Besides that, my background before my conversion was one of total unbelief."

The trio again laid hands upon me and prayed, this time for deliverance in my mind from all reservations and inhibitions. Then they prayed I'd have a free ability to speak with other tongues.

"That's enough," I said. "We've prayed for hours. It's apparent to me that this is not my time." They agreed, took their hands off my head and we all stood up to leave.

The top of my head seemed unusually hot when I stood up. My reaction was, "They've had their hands upon me so long my head is warm from their hands." But it did not go away. I recalled that the last time I had this sensation was following my conversion.

I thanked the men without telling them I was experiencing this "burning" or electric feeling, convinced that it would soon go away. But it didn't then—nor when I slipped into bed that night.

"Lord, are You trying to tell me that I have received the baptism with the Holy Spirit?" I prayed.

Then I recalled how I had earlier demanded tangible proof, *evidence* of the experience of receiving the baptism of the Holy Spirit. The Lord knew my doubting heart. The sensation I associated with my conversaion was proof that the Lord *was* indicating to me that indeed I did have this experience.

"Thank You, Lord. I accept this experience as from You," I said in my closing prayers that night.

I often had counseled with troubled people who were looking for an experience, usually peace or joy, to look to the Lord and His Word. Peace and joy would follow, I told them. I had learned in my ministry not to look for a *feeling* of anointing as a criterion that I'd be successful. Often wonderful things had happened *without any feeling on my part whatsoever.*

Our confidence must be in the Lord and His Word. Then as we act in faith, the Lord reveals His presence and power.

Moreover, if we look for emotional experiences, we usually are looking for the wrong thing. This is certainly true in salvation, and generally true in all advances in the faith. Occasionally, however, the Lord grants some tangible evidences because of the circumstances. I had not spoken in tongues, because I had not known what was involved in this gift. Yet the Lord graciously gave me a tangible physical experience as He had done when I was converted, apparently so I might associate the two.

Several weeks later in Minneapolis, we had an evangelism conference sponsored by our department of evangelism. During that conference, five ALC pastors who had received the baptism with the Spirit and had the gift of speaking with other tongues described their experiences.

"When you receive the baptism with the Spirit, then step out by faith," one pastor said. "Begin speaking in tongues. This is something that *you* do with the *cooperation* of the Holy Spirit. *You* must take the initiative. The Holy Spirit does not come to *possess* you, but to *empower* you. Saint Paul said, 'I pray with my mind and with my spirit,' indicating his will was involved when he spoke with his spirit, which I believe was his exercising the gift of speaking with other tongues."

This made sense to me. I believed he had put his finger on the crux of my own problem. A few days later I was alone in my study, and I prayed, "Lord, I do not know how to pray in tongues, but I believe I have received the Holy Spirit, so now I am going to speak in tongues."

I opened my mouth. This time I willfully tried to speak and I did! Freely, easily.

I *had* received the Holy Spirit, yet perhaps because of ignorance on my part, I did not know what to do. I saw that speaking in tongues is a matter of discovery. It is coming into a cooperation with the Holy Spirit so *you* can do something supernatural. And this is the key for all the other gifts of the Spirit. The truth became crystal clear. We are called to obey the Lord, have faith in His Word, then step out and believe that the Holy Spirit will cooperate with us. The Spirit brings to us power for healing, deliverance, and other miracles. We have the authority to use it—but we have to claim it before we can use it.

After the novelty of this gift wore away, my mind actively judged my experience. "It sounds so repetitious. What blessing can possibly come from this? I don't know what I am saying or even if I'm saying anything at all. I don't know if my spirit is praying or talking. How can this possibly benefit me?"

Then I found Paul's statement, "I thank God that I speak in tongues more than you all" (I Corinthians 14:18), and the promise, "One who speaks in a tongue, edifies himself" (I Corinthians 14:4).

I said, "I can't understand how I can edify myself with this gift of speaking with other tongues, but when Your Word says I'll edify myself, I'll believe it, no matter what my mind says. Lord, this gift involves no effort. I'm convinced it must be a form of rest and refreshment. So I'll use this gift, knowing I'll edify myself and that You'll give me rest and refreshment through its use. Thank you, Lord!"

But I found the gift of speaking in tongues causes stumbling for many Christians. They conceive this gift as being very bizzare, involving ecstasy or even hypnotic behavior. It is not that at all. This gift is usually an evidence of the presence and power of the Holy Spirit. It becomes, as it did to me, a revelation of how the Holy Spirit cooperates with a Christian in other ways. To speak in other tongues, you must take the initiative, expecting the cooperation of the Holy Spirit to do a supernatural thing—to speak in a language which your own mind cannot comprehend.

On the day of Pentecost, the Holy Spirit didn't speak through the one hundred and twenty people gathered in the upper room. The Bible says, *"They* began to speak as the Spirit gave them utterance" (Acts 2:4). In the healing ministry, the same principle is involved. A Christian empowered by the Spirit acts, using His will. He acts in faith toward God and in His Word. The Holy Spirit likewise cooperates with that person and does the supernatural work that brings about healing or a miracle.

The simplicity of this truth and the goodness of these gifts were still the subject of controversy in our denomination, however. I wondered what would happen in the days ahead if I began to use these gifts in my ministry. Could I use them—knowing the difficulties they might cause?

15

"I'LL EXPECT YOU
TO WORK MIRACLES"

In March 1962, I was holding meetings for eight days at Frontier, Saskatchewan, Canada. I came to this parish fresh from my new spiritual experience of receiving the baptism of the Holy Spirit.

The meetings went on as scheduled and brought forth good attendance each evening. Many of the parishioners were helped into an assured faith in Christ. During the day, the pastor and I made house calls and dealt with many in their own homes.

One day we pulled up to a farmstead. As we were ready to knock, the farmer met us at the door. His face was a mask of fright.

"My wife has just had a heart attack! She's in terrible pain. I was just about to call for the ambulance when you knocked! Please come in."

His wife was lying on the living room couch, groaning, white-faced, and in obvious pain.

"I'll call the doctor and the ambulance now!" said the farmer.

"Wait . . . let's pray first before you call," I said.

"Yes, of course, by all means," he said.

The pastor hesitated, thinking time was of the essence to get medical help to the woman. Yet he apparently sensed the need for immediate prayer, too.

He began, "Dear Lord Jesus, we come urgently to Your throne of mercy in behalf of our dear sister. We ask You to heal her, if it be Thy will."

The farmer prayed a quick and similar prayer. "Lord, if it be Thy will, heal my wife."

It was my turn. "Lord," I prayed, "we believe it *is* Your will to heal this dear woman." Then the Lord moved me strangely and I sensed an inner voice prompting me to add, "I lay hands upon her and *claim* healing for her in Jesus' name!"

Boldly, I laid my hands upon the forehead of the sick woman and did exactly what I had been prompted to do by the Spirit. Something happened immediately which all of us could see. The two men stood looking, wide-eyed. I was sursprised myself! The grimace left her face, her color returned. Her gasps subsided.

"The pain is all gone!" she said.

Her husband held the telephone receiver in his hand, uncertain. Then slowly, with a smile of relief spreading across his weatherbeaten face, he hung up the phone. We all knew the Lord had intervened. Still, there were attacks of doubt in my own mind.

The pastor prayed again. "Thank You, Lord, for delivering and healing our sister in Christ. Now we commit all things to Your care. In Jesus' name, Amen."

The farmer's wife was at the meeting that evening, radiant and exuding vibrant health. During the testimony time, she stood to her feet.

"This afternoon I was stricken with a heart attack. I felt as though I was dying. I was in such pain I could hardly think or pray. I asked the Lord quickly to send help. I was thinking about a doctor, but the Lord sent our pastor and Evangelist Mjorud. They prayed and Evangelist Mjorud laid hands upon me and in Jesus' name claimed healing. Immediately, I felt the power of God come over me. The pain disappeared and I was healed! All glory to God."

With such a miracle happening before my eyes and having her personal testimony, you would think that my own doubts would flee. But even after this testimony, I wasn't absolutely sure that a miracle had taken place. My mind kept saying, "It could have been gas pains, and they could have passed coincidentally just as I was praying."

Yet in my heart, my spirit assured me a miracle did happen. I found my mind indeed to be a battle ground. It's a big order "to bring every thought captive to obey Christ," as the Apostle Paul wrote.

Later that week while still at Frontier, a Lutheran missionary came to me for prayer in the late afternoon. Joyce Bergh was home on sick leave from Colombia, South America. She had driven over one hundred miles for help.

In talking with her, I observed that she had terrible psychological fears. When I asked about them, she confirmed my guess.

"These fears come upon me when I try to teach the Bible or give a message from God's Word. They got so bad that I had to leave the mission field. Besides this, I've become sick and weak. Pastor Mjorud, I've heard much about the 'baptism of the Holy Spirit.' I desire this blessing for myself. I know all of this is questioned by my superiors, both here in America and on the mission field. But I need this power to serve the Lord effectively in Colombia."

I counseled with Joyce. Then she prayed, asking the Lord to heal her body, deliver her from fears, and fill her with the Holy Spirit.

As I began to pray I felt an ungodly presence, almost as if I were contesting Satan and demonic spirits. I felt empowered suddenly by the Spirit of God.

"Unclean spirits, I command you to leave Joyce, in the name of Jesus Christ!" I said. I noticed her body relax from the stiff and rigid pose she was in.

"Lord, I claim healing for Joyce," I continued to pray. "In the power of the Spirit, completely restore her body. In the name of Jesus, stabilize her metabolism. Free her mind. Make her function as a whole person, healed. Lord, baptize Joyce with the Holy Spirit."

I told Joyce to receive the Holy Spirit by faith. Prayerfully, she did, thanking the Lord for His gracious gift to her.

"Now you can pray in a language you never learned," I said. "As I use this prayer language, you step out and do the same. You'll discover that the same Holy Spirit that is in me is in you."

I began praying with other tongues. She did the same. Her language was loquacious and linguistically beautiful.

In the process of praying for Joyce, I watched a woman being transformed before my very eyes. The wild fear in her eyes was gone. Her lined, drawn and distraught face became warm, smooth and beautiful! It was amazing. I'd never seen anything like it before.

We had been in the church and now went over to the parsonage next door. Joyce knew the pastor and his wife very well. When we came to the door, the minister's wife answered the bell.

"Joyce, what has happened to you!? Why, you look ten years younger!" she said.

When I was alone with my thoughts that night, I knew that God had positively worked a miracle in Joyce's life. There was no way my legal, sophisticated mind could rationalize this one away. I was puzzled. "Lord, what does this mean?" I asked. It occurred to me that the power of God *was* available for miracles today, just as it was when the book of Acts was taking place.

"All right, Lord," I prayed. "I'm convinced. I'll expect to see You work other miracles for Your glory."

And I did from time to time. Studying the Scriptures and seeing with new eyes the promises of God, my faith became stronger than ever. Many verses of Scripture burned in my heart with new meaning:

"I, the Lord, am your healer" (Exodus 15:26).

"And I will remove sickness from your midst" (Exodus 23:25).

"He Himself took our infirmities and carried away our diseases" (Matthew 8:17).

"And by His scourging we are healed" (Isaiah 53:5).

"Truly, truly, I say to you, if you shall ask the Father for anything, He will give it to you in my name" (John 16:23).

"They will lay hands on the sick and they will recover" (Mark 16:18).

These words in context with all Scripture in the realm of healing came alive. I incorporated these teachings in my proclamation of God's Word. People came forward for salvation as before. But mingled with them were many for healing, and the Lord was there to heal bodies as well as spirits. Pains vanished, arthritis went away, tumors disappeared, and many with heart ailments were healed.

I came to Belmond, Iowa. The meetings in the Lutheran Church were fruitful in every way. People found salvation. Others were healed. The Reverend Oscar Laveeg, pastor, was rejoicing at what was happening. He had one concern, however. He shared it with me.

"You've met Sid Swenson, our Adult Bible teacher."

I nodded.

The pastor continued. "Well, Sid knows the Bible very well. He holds the attention of the people and has a good result from his teaching. But Sid is rather negative. Our people aren't getting a positive understanding of the Gospel. Would you go to him and share what you know about victorious Christian living?"

"I would be glad to," was my reply.

Later that week, I made the call upon Sid Swenson as Laveeg had suggested. I had Sid's address, so I walked to his house. I rang the doorbell. Mrs. Swenson quickly answered the door. She was crying.

"Oh, Evangelist Mjorud! Please come in. Sid has just had a terrible heart attack! I've called the ambulance to take him to the hospital."

Inside I found Sid sprawled on the living room couch writhing in agonizing pain.

"Sid," I began earnestly, "do you believe what I have been saying these days on healing?"

"I believe anything that is in the Bible," Sid answered firmly, "and it's plain to me that healing is there."

"Do you believe that God *can* heal you and *wills* to heal you?" I asked further.

"Yes," he gasped. Catching his breath, he explained, "Before you came to Belmond, I knew the Lord *could* heal, but since you've come, I believe that he *wills* to heal, too. Especially since He brought you here right now."

"Let me lay hands upon you and pray for you," I offered. Without losing any time, I began praying, asking God to heal Sid.

As soon as I was through this simple prayer, Sid sat up. The pain was gone and he was breathing normally. He thanked the Lord in positive terms for healing his heart. Then he got to his feet, went to the phone, and canceled the ambulance!

"Let's have a cup of coffee," he said jubilantly after hanging up the phone.

Sid went into the kitchen and started pouring water into a kettle. His wife was still upset and confused. She tried to take over.

"Please get back on the couch and lie down. I think you're acting presumptuously."

Sid came back into the living room and instead of lying down, pulled up a chair next to mine.

"God has healed me this time," he said. "This has been my *third* heart attack! Believe me, this should have been the end for me. I was ready to meet the Lord, but I dreaded the thought of leaving my wife behind. I had just given my wife final instructions about finances so she'd know what to do when I died. Then you came!"

Many other miracles followed Sid's instantaneous healing. Not long after, I was in Ottawa, Illinois, for meetings in a Lutheran church. On the first afternoon, Mr. and Mrs. Carroll Nelson asked if I'd pray for their eleven-year-old daughter, Emily, one of seven children.

"Emily has been blind in her right eye for two years," the mother explained. "Her other eye has just five percent vision. It's going blind, too. We have had Emily to Mayo Clinic and the doctors tell us she has an incurable disease—and will be totally blind within six months. Will you pray for her and anoint her for healing?"

I was hesitant. In other healings, for the most part I had been an instrument of the Lord to *arrest* some physical problem. But here was a case where a young girl was totally blind in one eye and ninety-five percent blind in the other. Could I expect the Lord to *reverse* a physical process, rather than just arrest it? Doubts once again came to my mind. Bring sight to the blind? It might be too much to expect.

Then I was convicted by the Spirit of God. *This is not your doing. Nothing is too great for Me.* I was ashamed at almost projecting my own ego and doubts into this situation. It was true Herb Mjorud doesn't heal—God does. And nothing is too great. He can heal or cure heart trouble, appendicitis, psychological fears and just as easily heal blindness, or any "irreversible" problem.

I agreed to help and announced to the church I would hold a healing service for Emily and anoint her with oil. We invited others to come for healing, too. No one else came for healing, although many stayed to pray with us and to witness their first healing service. When the anointing service for Emily was over, Emily's mother said excitedly, "Emily, can you see? Can you see?"

"Not yet, Mother," Emily responded. "We take healing by faith."

Nothing that night indicated a miracle had taken place. I wondered if secretly my first thoughts were not right—that I should not have tried to pray for Emily's healing of blindness.

However, the next morning as Emily awoke, she saw a pinpoint of light from her blind eye! She put her hand up to cover her "good" eye and saw the fuzzy outline of the window. *She knew she was being healed!* From that point her eyes slowly kept mending. In six months, instead of being totally blind in both eyes as the doctors at Mayo Clinic had predicted, her eyes tested at total twenty/twenty vision.

I've seen Emily several times since her healing. Two years ago I was holding meetings in Forest City, Iowa, and Emily came. She was eighteen, tall, beautiful, with clear brown eyes— still with perfect vision!

Many quibble over the theological questions of healing. Instead they should think about the love of God demonstrated when He heals the eyes of an eleven-year-old girl, destined to be totally blind for a lifetime.

Not many months later, I was holding meetings in Albert Lea, Minnesota. I received a long distance call from Rochester, Minnesota. A friend from seminary days, the Reverend William Ostroot, was on the other end of the line.

"Herb," he informed me, "my wife is at Mayo Clinic for medical treatment. She's very sick. The doctors haven't diagnosed her ailment yet, but they think she inhaled some poisonous fumes. She's under an oxygen tent. Could you come by and pray for my wife?"

"Gladly," was my reply. "My wife and I will be driving back to Minneapolis in the morning. We'll come right over."

"Wonderful," was his relieved response. "See you then."

When my wife and I came to the foyer of the hospital, we met Pastor Ostroot. His eyes were red and swollen. It was obvious he hadn't slept all night.

"She's had a very uneasy night," he explained. "They took a biopsy of her lungs. That was major surgery in itself. The doctor informed me that her lungs were inflamed and poisoned. She is very seriously ill!"

"In that case we had better have a healing service for her right away," I urged. Turning to the chaplain, I invited him to come along and pray with us.

"I should say not!" he firmly retorted. "I'll have nothing to do with that healing ministry."

"All we are going to do is to take God's Word for what it says," I explained.

"I warn you," he said, "You'll destroy her faith."

"Why do you say that?"

"If she's *not* healed, she'll doubt that she has true faith in God. She'll have all kinds of spiritual doubts—maybe even lose her faith." With that he turned and left us. He was obviously no inspiration for us, but my wife, Pastor Ostroot and I took the elevator and soon were in his wife's room.

Mrs. Ostroot recognized us, but was very weak.

"Glad you have come," she said.

"We will have to pray with the oxygen tent over her," Pastor Ostroot advised.

We prayed, laid our hands on her body, one after the other, and claimed the promises of God's Word for healing. Then I anointed her head with a touch of olive oil, making the sign of the cross.

"I claim healing for you in the name of Jesus Christ!" I said.

Immediately Mrs. Ostroot appeared to dose off in sleep. We quietly left the room, chatted briefly with Pastor Ostroot, urging him to trust the Lord for a miracle. We then drove home to Minneapolis. Shortly after arriving home, the phone rang. It was Pastor Ostroot.

"My wife slept peacefully for two hours after you left," he said jubilantly. "And when she awoke, she was well! She pushed aside the oxygen tent and sat on the edge of her bed."

But in spite of her good physical condition, the doctors urged her to stay hospitalized and wait until the biopsy report came back from the lab. But since she insisted, and the Ostroots didn't live far from Rochester, the doctors allowed her to go.

Several days later, Mrs. Ostroot had an urgent call from Mayo's Clinic in Rochester. One of her doctors said, "Come to the clinic at once! We have the report from the laboratory and it is not good."

The Ostroots did not know what to make of this news. They drove to the clinic, were invited into an office and faced four doctors with very grave faces.

One of them spoke. "The biopsy has come back from the laboratory. The report reveals that you have cystic fibrosis of the lungs. Also, the doctor who took the biopsy noted during surgery that all visible parts of your lungs were black and infected. I'm afraid this is a very critical situation."

"Yes, but now I am perfectly well," Mrs. Ostroot said glibly. "I have been healed. I know I *was* very sick. But after a healing service, I fell asleep and woke two hours later healed and well. I removed the oxygen tent and even walked that afternoon."

"This is fantastic!" was the response of one of the doctors.

"By our reports, Mrs. Ostroot, you should still be under that oxygen tent fighting for your life. No doubt there has been a reversion."

"Yes," said another.

The third nodded. "God has undoubtedly intervened for you. We have seen these things happen before. Would you like us to perform surgery again to verify your miracle?"

"But that would be major surgery again, wouldn't it, Doctor?" Pastor Ostroot asked.

"Yes, the same as before," was his answer.

"But, I am feeling perfectly whole, doing all my house work, running up and down stairs as before I became ill. I don't see any point in having further surgery," Mrs. Ostroot argued. The Ostroots decided to return home. They did so with the doctors' consent.

"If you still had the disease, you'd be flat on your back, unable to breathe without oxygen," one doctor said, shrugging. "Go ahead and go home."

This miracle is but a link in a long chain. I have kept no running account of what the Lord has done, but I have received many letters and heard hundreds of testimonies.

The Lord does great things through one who has faith in His Word, who has been anointed by His Holy Spirit, who is obedient to Jesus Christ as Lord. Many followers of Jesus Christ in our day are finding a ministry of power and miracles. This has a primary purpose of bringing people everywhere to recognize that God is alive and at work today on planet earth. There is a tremendous drawing power in miracles to bring people to meetings where they can hear the Word of God. Clearly the greatest miracle is still the miracle of the new birth. However, we cannot minimize the blessing that comes to a person stricken with injury or disease who is healed by a personal touch from the Lord.

I preached in a different Lutheran church every week except the time each month I had off for rest and study. I felt obligated to inform each pastor of my experience in the Holy Spirit immediately upon meeting him. With some pastors there was a negative reaction against this gift. However, my main message in preaching was the message of sin and grace, with the view of bringing repentance, salvation, and assured faith to my hearers.

In most places, however, reports of healing miracles and the baptism of the Spirit preceded my coming. Therefore, many people came to the evangelistic meetings seeking healing and the baptism with the Spirit. I felt obliged to pray for the sick and for the baptism of the Spirit for those who sought it. In every church there would be some healed and some receiving the baptism with the Spirit.

I also felt I had to preach at least one message on the Holy Spirit, that this power might be put into Scriptural perspective and come with its revival power.

In one congregation where we held meetings for eight days, we held a special healing service one afternoon with twenty-five to thirty coming for that service. There were many instant healings that day. By the middle of that week, people also came freely for the baptism with the Spirit. Some lingered after the services. Others came during the day to the pastor's study.

After that series of meetings, the pastor wrote to report that there had been no trouble in his church since the advent of the baptism with the Holy Spirit. He also reported the wonderful numerical and spiritual growth, the outpouring of the Spirit upon the youth, and the general fantastic impact his people were having upon the whole community.

However, there were storm clouds on the horizon for me.

16

HOSTILITY TO THE WORK
OF THE HOLY SPIRIT

Throughout the week of one of my most successful campaigns, I noticed that a number of Lutheran pastors from neighboring parishes were visiting our meetings. I knew from speaking to one that there was open hostility to the ministry of the Holy Spirit.

When I returned to Minneapolis my director called me into his office. "Mjorud, do you know what this is?"

He handed me some papers to read. I looked at them carefully. I could hardly believe what I read.

"Looks like a copy of formal charges of heresy being brought against me!" I said.

They were signed by the minister who had opposed my ministry in that last parish. My director was upset. He waved the report at me, asking for an explanation.

"These charges are completely false," I said.

He showed me other letters of complaint by other pastors. I read with growing discomfort and dismay.

"Look, Mjorud. You're an evangelist. Leave these matters of the Holy Spirit alone. It will only lead to trouble," he said. "Our Lutheran Church is not ready for these things."

I understood his concern and could not blame him for his reaction after reading the negative criticisms of what I was doing.

"Those charges of heresy are patently false," I asserted. "I will be glad to answer those charges in writing or in public hearings."

He answered, "That one letter really contains formal charges. It would be well for you to answer them in writing—before any *trial* should come up!"

"I'll do it . . . and make copies for you, the district president, and the president of our denomination," I volunteered.

"Do that. In the meantime be very careful about promoting the gifts of the Spirit. They only cause trouble wherever they appear."

"If you feel I ought to leave the Lutheran Church, I'll do so at your word," I offered.

"No, we don't want you to leave. You are too valuable as an evangelist. You are gifted in this way like no other man we have in the Lutheran Church," he said. "But your involvement in the charismatic ministry is not understood."

I was convinced I had found an answer for spiritual renewal and outreach for the Lutheran Church. Now I was told it "did not fit" and that I had "better leave it alone." The easy way would be to give in—to leave out the charismatic ministry and its power. I had enough trouble—humanly speaking—simply preaching salvation and an assured faith. But I was convinced I had received the charismatic ministry from the Lord as the answer to my search for the key to spiritual renewal. To me it was something so plainly revealed in the Scriptures that I wondered how Christian leaders could have escaped it in the past.

I answered the formal charges of heresy point by point in writing. On his own, and knowing nothing about these charges against me, the pastor of that congregation where I had conducted these so-called "heretical" meetings, went to the president of the ALC. He gave him a firsthand report of the marvelous things that had happened in his parish through my ministry. Having my letter and this report, the president wrote a letter to the accusing pastor and the charges were dropped.

I continued my ministry from parish to parish, and wherever I went, souls were finding peace with God through an assured faith. Plainly, since receiving the baptism with the Spirit, my ministry was proving more effective than ever before.

However, every time I returned to Minneapolis, I'd get a heavy heart. I knew more unfavorable reports about my new ministry would be on the desk of my superior. It got so I dreaded to call or see my director. He'd either read new letters to me or have me read them. Some were vitriolic. It was apparent that many were not writing from actual firsthand evidence, but from what they *imagined* I was doing. Some letters were outright false accusations. I could easily disprove them, but it was time consuming to be constantly putting out these "brush fires."

One day I was called down to my director's office. "We have an appointment together to see the president of the Church," he said.

We went to his office. There my director read a long letter from a pastor whom he described as "one of the most prominent and respected pastors in the American Lutheran Church." That letter contained the cruelest attack ever made upon me in my life. It was bitter, critical, with half truths and outright lies. It contained only what some people *wanted to believe about me.*

I prayed, "Lord, I'm weary of defending myself. This time I will not say one word on my behalf. *You* are my vindication."

So I remained silent although I knew that silence was tantamount to an admission of guilt. But I had taken my stand. I gave the problem to the Lord and said nothing.

As we walked down the stairwell to the next floor, my director angrily said, "Mjorud, I warned you to have nothing to do with that healing ministry!"

As he spoke I recalled that I had conducted a healing service for him a short time before at which he acknowledged a healing intervention from the Lord.

"I recall when you were sick and grasping for straws. You had no hesitation in having me anoint you with oil and lay hands upon you for *your* healing!" I said. "Every week I see sick people in a helpless condition. My Bible tells me, 'If you know how to do good, and do not do it, for you it is sin.' "

The director flushed.

"Forgive me, Herb. I have spoken presumptuously."

Nothing more was said that day. But I left him sensing more trouble was brewing.

It seemed that while I was conducting meetings, everything moved along smoothly. However, when I left, conflict would develop in most parishes where I had been. Those who had received the baptism with the Spirit witnessed to others in the parish, urging them to share their experience. This came across as a "holier than thou" attitude, and friction resulted between the "haves" and "have nots." No doubt there was fault on both sides, but the baptism in the Holy Spirit became an acute problem in some churches. Several schisms came as a consequence.

Again I was called in and reprimanded by my co-workers and superiors in the ALC. Again I was warned to have nothing to do with the charismatic ministry. I felt trapped, certain that God had given me the "go" sign. But my respected co-workers were giving me just the opposite.

I prayed all the more and sensed that the Lord continued to direct me in every move. This was a tremendous relief to me, for my troubles with the Lutheran Church seemed impossible from a human viewpoint.

I didn't understand why there should be opposition. Then the Lord revealed to me that I would not be serving much longer in my present position. His Word, "Any door that a man opens to you can be closed by men, but the door that I will soon open for you, no man can close," seemed directed to me.

Personally, I could not understand how the ALC could keep me when I was so unpopular and the subject of so much criticism. My term of six years was about to expire. I realized they were probably just letting my call expire. I was asked to appear before them. Designated officials questioned me about my "charismatic activity." Next, they requested that a meeting of the staff of evangelists be called to discuss the problem.

That next meeting with twelve co-workers was most difficult. For six hours they begged me to give up my healing involvement. To most of these men, my ministry was clandestine—not in keeping with Lutheran theology or with the interpretation which the ALC held on this present Holy Spirit movement.

After long and fruitless discussions, one of the men said, "I am prepared to give a Bible study on the gifts of the Holy Spirit as outlined in I Corinthians 12. Let's see what the Bible teaches on this subject. After all, this is the reason Mjorud is having trouble."

But another was vehemently opposed to this approach. He said loudly, "Our Church has acted through an appointed committee to study these gifts. This study committee has given our Church guidelines. Those guidelines specifically say that these gifts are *not to be promoted in our churches.* Mjorud *is* promoting these gifts. He's going contrary to what the Church has approved. There is no point in studying the Scriptures on this issue. Mjorud will either have to change his tactics or leave!"

There appeared no room for further discussion, but to make certain, the next remarks ended that matter. Another evangelist said, "I have made up my mind. If Mjorud does not leave the Commission on Evangelism, *I* will leave!"

Still another hit was given below the belt: "I think Mjorud was the reason our director has had so much trouble and anxiety. I believe Mjorud's activities were the primary cause of his sickness!"

The director came quickly to my rescue on this accusation, however. "My sickness was cancer! That is not psychosomatic. Any undue stress I may have had had nothing to do with Mjorud."

Most of the six hours of that meeting were spent trying to clarify the rumors which these men had heard about my ministry. It was amazing to me that reasonable men would even believe that a brother in Christ would become involved in the activities such wild rumors depicted.

At the close of this meeting, I was addressed by one of the senior evangelists. "Mjorud, we know that you are a called man of God. We know that you have the gift of evangelism. There is no one who is better qualified than you to preach repentance and salvation. We *need* you for this in our denomination. Now leave off this charismatic ministry, on a trial basis—for one year. Give us your word to this and we will recommend you to the Commission on Evangelism, and you can continue your ministry with us."

My decision was most difficult to make. I loved these men, had long respected them as brothers in Christ. We had years of fellowship and ministry together. I looked at each of the twelve men around the table. I spoke slowly and carefully.

"I know I can do what you are asking. I can do a good job with the use of the human talent God has given me. But the Lord said, 'If any man puts his hand to the plow and turns back, I will have no pleasure in him.' That's exactly what you're asking me to do. That's a sacrifice I cannot make. Though I can minister and even win men's commendation, I won't have the good pleasure of God behind me. I have to continue in what I know and have experienced, no matter what the cost is to me personally!"

There was no reason to continue the meeting after that. The director shook his head sadly and asked for someone to pray. Many of the men were in tears, for we all knew this meant that my ministry with the ALC was at an end.

A series of eerie circumstances followed that meeting. These events seemed more than coincidental, as though God were speaking to His servants who were hostile toward the gifts of the Spirit, especially the gift of healing.

The evangelist who opposed judging my ministry on the basis of a Bible study had a heart attack while boarding a bus immediately following that meeting. He died three months later.

The evangelist who begged me to drop my Holy Spirit ministry and continue with them was stricken while on his next assignment. He has been incapacitated ever since.

Two more were stricken with heart attacks shortly after our meeting.

All this prompted our director to write in a letter to his staff, "Is the Lord trying to say something to us by this sudden rash of sicknesses on our staff?"

Later, the Commission on Evangelism was eliminated by official action of the ALC.

I had no malice in my heart towards these men. They were brothers in Christ and fellow servants of Jesus Christ. But like so many others, they were equating loyalty to Lutheran dogma with loyalty to Jesus Christ. I was not fighting Lutheran doctrine; I believed it to be a true expression of Biblical truth. But I also believed with conviction that the gifts of the Holy Spirit also were valid, and were meant to supplement what we already held to be true.

One more opportunity remained. I could appear before the Church Council for review of the decision of the Commission on Evangelism. But I knew this was futile, as I was told by the Lord. But God led me to appear anyway, to witness what the Spirit of God was doing.

When I was called into their meeting, the president suggested I speak for a half hour in defense of my ministry. Then, he said, questions could be asked during a second half hour.

In informal remarks I witnessed to them of my reception of the baptism with the Spirit.

"I'll refer to some supernatural events that have taken place in my ministry. None of these is reported for my credit, but for the glory of God. The credit goes solely to His Spirit," I said.

I spent the remainder of the time referring to people—Lutherans for the most part—giving names and addresses for corroborating purposes. These people had been demonstrably healed—one of diabetes, two of heart attacks, one of blindness, one of a cystic fibrosis in her lungs, and several others—all healed supernaturally and with doctor's verifications.

During the question time, one district president reported that congregations in his district where I had been were experiencing difficulties. He added, "I cannot believe that this Holy Spirit ministry is of God."

Another district president asked the question, "What happened in Clarkfield?"

I knew exactly what he was referring to. With some

reluctance but out of necessity, I detailed what happened in Clarkfield, Minnesota, in the Clarkfield Lutheran Church. This incident caused me more trouble than any other situation in my ministry. I knew that was the reason beind the Church Council questions.

"I fully realize that what I am about to report is subjective in nature and open to many points of view," I began. "I am sure you are aware of other incidents where a person has been pronounced dead by a doctor, and then has revived. Such things have happened before. All I want to do is to report what I did and what I observed. You may draw your own conclusions.

"At the closing of an evening service, I asked those who sought salvation to pray silently for forgiveness. I suggested that those who wanted to receive Jesus Christ as Savior raise their hands. Many hands came up immediately. But one woman in a back pew raised her hand, then dropped it rather limply, as though she had fainted. Another woman, whom I learned later was a registered nurse, quickly went to her aid," I continued.

The full Council was listening attentively now.

"But I was preoccupied with the invitation. Hands kept coming up. Nearly forty-five people raised their hands to receive Christ. I had prayer, words of instruction, and turned the service over to the pastor for closing. We sang a closing hymn, he pronounced the benediction, then asked me to join him behind the choir to greet people at the door on their way out."

One of the Council members shifted in his seat. His movements suggested, get to the point, Mjorud.

"About half way through this farewell ceremony at the door," I went on, "a woman pressed through the crowd to me. She was crying. 'Oh, Pastor Mjorud,' she begged, 'please come and help us. Mrs. Ford is either dying or dead. Come and pray with us!'

"I left the handshaking and headed immediately to the back pew. Two nurses were standing behind Mrs. Ford who had slumped into the pew. As I slipped into the pew in front of Mrs.

Ford, one nurse shook her head (to alert me but not upset Mr. Ford) as if to say, 'There's nothing you can do.'

"Someone said, 'Mrs. Ford has fainting spells.'

" 'Yes, I know,' the registered nurse said. 'She has had many fainting spells, but when you have a fainting spell, there's a heartbeat. Mrs. Ford doesn't have a heartbeat.'

"I did not know what to do and prayed for God's help. The Spirit of God began to move upon me—again I can't demonstrate this to you—it's just an awareness you know. I put my hand upon Mrs. Ford's face. It was cold and clammy. I put the back of my hand under her nose to feel for a breath. I could feel none. I picked up her loose arm to feel for a pulse. Nothing. I waited to sense a heartbeat; again the nurse shook her head."

The men were quiet, even respectful as I continued my account.

"I told the people in the back of the church that Mrs. Ford had passed on,' adding, 'But what a wonderful place and way to leave, right here in church, among her friends and loved ones.'

"But suddenly, with those words, the Spirit of God spoke to me: 'What did Paul do when Eutychus fell in the synagog and was picked up dead? I recalled what Paul did. He prayed for that man and he came back to life.

"Then I did something without thinking. I stretched out my hand and put it on Mrs. Ford and prayed, 'This is for the glory of God. Nothing is impossible with us who believe in Jesus Christ. It is a very simple thing for You, O Lord, to bring our dear sister back to life. Lord, reveal Your glory and restore life to this woman.'

"I felt something happening in her body. I put my hand again to her face. This time I could sense an ever-so-slight breath. 'Mrs. Ford is breathing,' I said.

"The nurse picked up her arm then said, 'She can't be breathing, because there is no pulse beat.'

"Then Mrs. Ford's chest began to heave and I said, 'She *is* breathing. Look at her chest.'

" 'That must be some kind of reflex action,' the nurse suggested, 'because there still is no heartbeat . . . . Wait! Wait a minute. Her heart has started! Now her pulse is beating!'

"Then Mrs. Ford opened her eyes and said, 'Oh, I've got to go home.'

" 'You can't go home yet,' the nurse said. 'We have called the doctor and the ambulance.'

" 'Oh, I'm all right,' Mrs. Ford said to the nurse. Turning to me, she shook my hand and said calmly, 'Thank you, Pastor Mjorud, for that very wonderful sermon.'

"Then the doctor came. He took out his stethoscope and listened to Mrs. Ford's heart. He checked her pulse, took a pen light and looked into her eyes and said finally, 'There is nothing wrong with you, Mrs. Ford. You can go home.' So she did. I had a number of people waiting down in front of the church to counsel with me so I said good night to Mrs. Ford and went to work again."

There was a lot more I could have told the Council— but didn't. For example, I could have said, "There's more. The next day in school, one of the fourth graders in 'show and tell' reported of 'seeing a woman raised from the dead.' The teacher called the pastor and asked, 'Is there anything to this?'

" 'A very strange thing *did* happen,' the pastor told her. 'From all outward circumstances that is exactly what appeared to happen. I was there.'

" 'What did the doctor say? You can't have wild reports like this flying around without medical proof,' the teacher said excitedly to the pastor.

"The pastor checked with the doctor. The doctor asked how long Mrs. Ford was unconscious without a heartbeat. The pastor guessed the time to be about fifteen minutes. The doctor said her heart could not stop that long without doing irreparable brain damage.

"When I met the pastor that evening, he said, 'Mrs. Ford's heart could not have stopped for that much time, or her brain would have been damaged.'

" 'How long was Lazarus dead?' was my quick answer. 'When the Lord does a miracle, we can't use human standards of judgment.' "

However, I did tell the Council that, strangely, what

happened to Mrs. Ford was not a source of blessing, but a topic for controversy in the church and that community.

When I finished my report of this incident, the district president asked, "Did you know Mrs. Ford suffered from fainting spells before that night in Clarkfield?"

"Yes, I already told you someone made an allusion to that before I prayed for her. You'll remember the nurse said this was not a fainting spell because there was no heartbeat."

I knew these men were thinking I had prayed for a fainting woman and naively thought God had raised her from the dead. Subsequent reports substantiated this.

I had thought through the circumstances surrounding Mrs. Ford's recovery over and over again. It would have obviated all kinds of trouble if I had merely gone along with this popular opinion. Everyone was waiting for me to say, "Mrs. Ford fainted and she revived after I prayed for her." But, I was there! In good conscience I could not do that. Both of the nurses who attended Mrs. Ford pronounced her dead. We all believed then, as well as later, that she had been literally raised from the *dead.* Granted, no physician was there with medical instruments to examine her until after she revived. But when I examined her in my superficial way, I believed that she was dead. I believed the Holy Spirit also knew her to be dead. The Holy Spirit led me to do what Paul did when he raised Eutychus from the dead. In my mind, *she was dead.* My prayer was not for her to come out of a fainting spell, but that the Lord would bring *back her life.*

I actually *felt* life come back into her body with my hands upon her. All who were there, the nurses, the husband, her relatives, the pastor, and even Mrs. Ford herself, believed she had actually been raised from the dead.

I have had supernatural intervention in my life, time and time again. *I believe this to be normal for a Christian.* We who are Christians say we believe in a supernatural God who can do anything. We believe that when we invoke the name of Jesus Christ, we have His actual presence. But do we expect Him to do anything above the natural? Many believers go through entire lifetimes with few, if any, supernatural events in their lives.

To become a Christian, there has to be supernatural intervention. The Spirit of God touches the spirit of man, giving that spirit eternal life. How strange such a person then denies that Jesus Christ, by the same Spirit, can work miracles in the physical realm, touching the body and the mind to heal. Doubt and unbelief, caused by centuries of teaching and instruction, prevent Christians from believing that miracles and healing are for today.

The men took a vote after I was excused. Unanimously, they decided not to extend my call as an evangelist for the American Lutheran Church.

As I drove home that day, believing that I would be rejected, I wondered what God had in store for me.

17

THE MYSTERY OF HEALING

I left the meeting with my denominational leaders with my mind a jumble of inner conflicts.

Reviewing what happened, I realized I could easily have stayed with the commission by conceeding to their requests "to have nothing to do with the gifts of the Holy Spirit." I still would have had an open door to reach souls for Jesus Christ. And I'd have had financial security.

However, giving up my ministry with the power gifts of the Holy Spirit to please men would be compromise. I would be successful in their eyes, but a failure in the eyes of God. The Lord wanted my obedience. His Word commanded me to "preach His Word." That meant I must declare all of that message, holding back nothing which I believed was revealed to me.

I had no fear about financial security. I left that behind when I gave up the practice of law for the "gamble" of commercial fishing, trusting God to meet our needs. I had long ago claimed the promise of Philippians 4:19: "And my God will supply every need of yours according to His riches in glory in Christ Jesus."

I chose to obey the Lord. I was convinced my decision was right, although I also knew what results would follow my decision.

The president of the American Lutheran Church wrote me to inform me the Church Council sustained the decision of the Commission on Evangelism. Officially, I was no longer an evangelist of the Church. I wrote to Lutheran churches scheduled for my meetings in 1965 and informed them my term was expiring, that I no longer was an evangelist in the Church. All churches but one cancelled out! I had only one meeting scheduled for 1965.

I put my law training to good use and filed incorporation papers. Three Lutheran pastors and one Lutheran layman agreed to serve on the board of trustees for the newly formed *Mjorud Evangelistic Association.*

After the cancellation of my bookings, I had a long distance call from Dr. Ted Sahlstrom, an optometrist from Albany, Oregon. "Herb, can you come to Portland and hold a series of meetings?"

"Yes, I am free to go anywhere," I replied.

"Give me a date and I will set up a city-wide crusade for you," he said.

"How about the second week in February?" I asked.

"That'll be fine," he said. "I'll call you again in a few days."

With that, he went to Portland, contacted about twenty Christian businessmen, formed a crusade committee, and rented a hall in downtown Portland. He began working on publicity and advertising.

I received calls from two Lutheran pastors in California. I set up meetings in both churches prior to going to Portland. The day after I had incorporated, I was on the road with meetings lined up for the next three weeks. The meetings at Fremont and San Jose Lutheran churches were good. The Holy Spirit worked powerfully in both. There seemed to be a new liberty in my ministry. I no longer feared a confrontation with superiors when I returned to headquarters. My present board, all men who had experienced the baptism with the Holy Spirit, would welcome any report of people saved, healed, and filled with the Spirit.

The crusade in Portland, interdenominational in character, was well attended. There were twenty-one conversions the first evening. Miracles of new life, physical and spiritual healings were evidenced.

During the crusade, the Spirit of God impressed on me the need to select a man to set up additional meetings in other cities. And the man who set up the Portland crusade committee appeared to be the one whom the Lord wanted. Humanly speaking, however, His choice did not seem possible. Dr. Sahlstrom had an active practice in optometry. I let him know anyway.

"Ted, I sense the Spirit of God leading me to ask you to help set up additional crusades even as you've done here in Portland," I said.

His eyes filled with tears. With a voice breaking with emotion, he said, "I can hardly believe this. It's like a dream! The Lord also has spoken to me about serving Him across the United States somehow. Now He's spoken to you. How can I turn Him down?"

So Dr. Ted Sahlstrom became my first assistant. Soon he was traveling across America. He not only set up crusades but always was present at the meetings. He spoke, counseled and had a hand in a personal ministry to individuals, with many conversions, healings, and Christians receiving the baptism with the Spirit. Meanwhile, he still carried on his profession. Patients were booked solid in his office the days he was home.

What happened in our meetings?

In the third Portland crusade, two years after starting this new ministry, thirty-five where converted the first night. About the same number came forward for healing. On the second night, a man came forward with his wife to give his testimony. I had prayed with them in the hospital a year before. He had fallen from a telephone pole as a line man, hitting his head on the pavement. At the hospital, examining doctors gave him up. They told his wife that he was a hopeless case. But his wife insisted the doctors do what they could. She went into the chapel to pray. The doctors reluctantly performed cranial surgery, removing parts of his skull to relieve the pressure when his injured brain expanded.

When I visited him in the hospital, he had been unconscious

for three months. The doctors had said he'd never regain consciousness. His wife had called me, so I prayed with her, anointing her husband with oil.

The next day she called me, and excitedly said, "My husband regained consciousness! He can't speak—the doctors already told me he'd never speak again. But he's conscious!"

I went back three days later and again prayed for him. Immediately he began to speak! Still the doctors gave them no hope.

"I'm sorry, but you'll never walk again. And, obviously, you'll never work again," said one of the physicians.

But the man and his wife believed the Lord would continue to work miracles. And He did. That evening in the meeting this young man stood tall and confident as he testified from the platform.

"I'm praising God! Through His power, I'm not only walking, but I'm back at work! There's nothing too hard for God."

That same night, another man was at the meeting. We learned later that he'd been brought against his will. He had gotten up to leave several times, but it seemed he could not go. Finally, he came to the altar.

"I'm not saved. I need the Lord," he said.

I noticed he had a stiff neck and asked him about it.

"I broke my neck in an accident. Four of the vertebrae are fused, and my neck is stiff with constant and terrible pain," he explained.

I counseled with him, and he accepted Jesus as His personal Savior. Then I laid hands upon him and prayed for his healing. When I took my hands off his head, he stared at me in utter amazement.

"Why, it's unbelievable! My pain is gone!"

He twisted his head sideways and up and down. "Look, I now can move my head. The doctors told me I'd have this stiffness the rest of my life."

The following evening many more testified to healings. This is what we saw and experienced in all our city-wide crusades.

In Portland, we set up follow-up teaching meetings for those who received the baptism in the Holy Spirit. This turned out to be a very helpful practice. Capable men and women from all walks of life who came out of that first Portland crusade are now serving the Lord.

But we soon learned of a problem happening in some of the cities. People who received the baptism with the Spirit and belonged to denominational churches were ostracized from local congregations. They'd return after their experience and testify of it to their pastor. Soon they were cut off from teaching Sunday School or holding an office in the church. They were forbidden to do what they, by the Spirit, became qualified to do. Some were so castigated they left their churches. Then came the criticism that the baptism of the Spirit made unfaithful church members. Many of these Spirit-filled people, out of self-defense, retreated into hibernation. Without fellowship and teaching, spiritual stagnation set in.

Because of this, I saw it would be more advantageous to establish a Christian community of like-minded people who could band themselves together and allow the Holy Spirit to do His work through them.

The last large crusade was scheduled for the Seattle Center in Washington. Shortly before the crusade week, however, while in Minneapolis, I agreed to a separate meeting on a Friday evening at the Minnehaha Lutheran Church. The auditorium was filled. Many made decisions for Christ. And many came forward either for healing or baptism in the Spirit. A number of trained counselors who had worked in a crusade which I conducted in Minneapolis the year before were there to help me.

After the services and counseling, some of the workers stayed for prayer. One of them said, "Let's all gather around Reverend Mjorud. We need to pray for him and his coming crusades in Seattle and Vancouver."

Grateful for their prayerful interest, I gladly knelt at the altar rail. They surrounded me in prayer, with those nearest placing their hands on me. One after another prayed.

While in this spirit of prayer, one man began to prophecy. (Prophesy is another of the gifts of the Holy Spirit. It is given by a Spirit-anointed Christian who speaks a message under the direct inspiration of the Spirit.)

The substance of his prophecy was, "You soon will be sent upon the mission for which the Lord, your God, has been training you. You shall travel all around the world to many nations declaring the whole counsel of God to people of many backgrounds and tongues. Nations that do not know you will call you. The Lord, your God, shall send you to nations you do not know. But be not afraid. He who has called you will be with you, to uphold you."

These words burned in upon my heart and mind, and gripped my soul. I was aware that this would be in direct fulfillment of my own call from God's written word (Isaiah 55:5) when the Holy Spirit personalized those words to me nine years before!

No one there, of course, knew of that prior experience. I told Bert Bauman, the man used of the Spirit to speak that message. "This prophecy is very significant to me."

"I'm glad to hear you say that," Bert replied. "When those words came out of my mouth, I thought that it was all rather farfetched."

I pondered the message. Travel around the world for the Lord? *When? How? Where?* I was so moved I could hardly stand up after we were through praying.

Soon after, I was on my way to Vancouver and Seattle. I spent several days with the crusade committee and held sessions with the personal workers. One morning, at my prayer time, the Lord revealed that I was to receive a very different call that day. It was to be a call for which I'd have to come to Him for guidance.

At a luncheon that day I spoke to twenty pastors interested in the crusade. Fred Doerflein, the crusade chairman, was supposed to be at that luncheon, but failed to arrive. Business had detained him and he arrived after the meeting ended. Fred ordered lunch, and I sat down with him to go over crusade details.

When we finished, Fred turned to me.

"I have something else to take up with you. There's a group

of fifteen or more Full Gospel Businessmen taking a tour around the world. We plan to preach and witness wherever we have opportunity. It'll be a thirty-two-day trip. We need an official evangelist to accompany us. And we all agree that you are the man! We don't have money for your fare, but we're trusting the Lord to provide it!"

Was this the call the Lord had in mind? That night I prayed earnestly. The answer I received from the Lord was, "This is it; accept that call."

I phoned Fred Doerflein and let him know my decision.

"Each member of the tour must deposit one thousand six hundred and fifty dollars by the fifteenth of January," Fred said. "Our tickets and hotel bills have to be prepaid."

"I don't know where that money will come from," I said. "But as you say, the Lord will provide. Let's trust Him for it."

On the last evening of that Seattle crusade, after a long time of personal counseling and prayer with a number of people, I noticed a woman sitting alone. Thinking that she needed help, I went across the auditorium to her.

"Is there something I can do for you?" I asked.

She looked directly at me and explained, "My husband died last year. We have a farm. Since he has been gone, I've rented out the land."

She opened her purse, took out a folded piece of paper and continued her story.

"I received this check, which represents my share of the net profits. The Lord seemed to say to me that this money was to be used for missions. I set it aside. Weeks went by. Finally, I felt I had to do something about that money. I sat down and asked the Lord what I should do with it. I believe the Lord wants you to have it."

"That's most generous. You should know that I am trusting God for the funds for a missionary trip around the world. I need one thousand six hundred and fifty dollars."

She looked down at the check and then at me. Her eyes widened in amazement as she unfolded it. The check was made out for one thousand six hundred and fifty dollars!

There were nineteen of us on that evangelistic tour. The Lord opened doors in London, Rome, the Holy Land, Bombay, Vijayawada, Hyderabad, Madras, Colombo, Jaffna, Djakarta, Hong Kong, Honolulu, and several other cities. I preached thirty-nine times, to small groups and to crowds as large as twelve thousand. There are many highlights, but I think of the first meeting in India where seven thousand had gathered. I preached and gave the call to receive Jesus Christ as Savior. Over half of the people raised their hands!

They must have misunderstood me or my interpreter, I thought, so I went over the invitation again as clearly as possible. I once again asked those who wanted to receive Christ to stand. About half of them stood, three thousand five hundred people! They all recited a prayer of repentance after my interpreter. The crowd eventually grew to twelve thousand—and I preached every night.

One evening was set aside for healing prayer. Our entire team, plus national pastors and evangelists, were used for this purpose. Thousands were prayed for. I wondered how effective such a mass service could be.

In Hyderabad I preached several nights in a large Methodist church. When I gave an altar call for those wanting spiritual help, more than one hundred came forward.

We all had a chance to testify, preach, counsel and pray for the sick on that trip. Hundreds, then thousands responded to the invitations to accept Jesus Christ as Savior. We talked first with those wishing to accept Christ, then with those wishing healing.

It is still a mystery to me how I can pray for a group of people whom I do not know, and some are saved and healed and others are not. As far as I know, I pray with the same compassion and faith for each one. Some are healed instantly. Others show no visible sign of healing at the time, but are later healed or made well. And some are not healed at all. These things are an enigma to all who are involved in a healing ministry. We know, however, that the Lord knows all the circumstances behind every case. Often a delay or absence of healing brings a spiritual blessing.

Although not everyone who is prayed for at a meeting is

healed, there always are some who are healed, revealing the presence and power and compassion of our Lord Jesus Christ. He is the healer—we are just instruments. He said signs would follow those who believe. (See Mark 16:17-20.)

Now I could see that my background, education, training and experiences were all geared toward this unique ministry. Today the world evangelistic tours are about one hundred days in length. I have now been on eight of them. We prepare and pray for these remarkable journeys *expecting* God to bless in amazing, miraculous ways. And we are never disappointed.

18

MIRACLES IN SRI LANKA

The tiny island nation of Ceylon now is called the Republic of Sri Lanka. One my first visit to Sri Lanka, I saw how little impact the Gospel had made there. Only three percent of the population was even nominally Christian; eighty percent were Buddhist, ten percent Hindu, and another seven percent comprised all other religions.

Our first meetings there were small, but the Lord placed a burden on my heart for this country. After the first missionary journey, our greatest concentration of effort has been in this island.

Five years ago I was ministering there in the city of Kandy which is aptly called "the Buddhist capital of the world." In the center of this large city is the Buddhist "Temple of the Tooth." Buddhists believe they actually found a tooth from Buddha himself. They enshrined this tooth in a large sarcophagus and built a huge temple to house the sarcophagus.

One day as I was holding meetings in the city of Kandy, evangelists Jacob Perera and Verghese Chandy, nationals of Sri Lanka, were praying with me in my hotel room. We all had a deep concern for reaching this pagan land for Christ. During prayer, the Lord gave me a vision of a stream of water falling upon this city and flowing out in many streams in all directions throughout the island.

We concluded this meant the Lord wanted to do a work in the city of Kandy where the "living waters" of the Gospel would flow in all directions. We often talked about starting a Bible school to train gospel workers. But we didn't know where to locate such a school. From this vision, we concluded the Lord directed us to the city of Kandy.

Some Swedish missionaries had the same desire to start a Bible school. Later, together with them, Lanka Bible Institute was opened. Our evangelistic association in America supplied them with funds to finance the school. The school is now well established, with more than forty graduates now serving the Lord.

My first visits to Sri Lanka had me traveling to many places with many small meetings, but with signal success in seeing many converted to Christ. I also saw the miracle of God's hand at work to heal and fill with the Spirit.

A very dramatic change came, however, in 1973. Evangelist Eivind Froen from Norway, my traveling partner, and I arrived in Colombo, Sri Lanka on March 5. Native co-workers informed us that this night was the opening meeting of an eight-day crusade featuring Evangelist Argemiro from Brazil. Most of the Christian churches in Colombo were cooperating for this crusade. I had never heard of Evangelist Argemiro, but at the insistence of my co-workers both Evangelist Froen and I attended that meeting. It was an open air meeting in the park grounds with about eight thousand people present. Evangelist Argemiro preached in English with an interpreter. He was a good preacher and capably expounded the Scriptures.

Many posters throughout the city announced that at this meeting, Evangelist Argemiro would pray specifically for the deaf and dumb. Printed leaflets urged people to bring deaf and dumb friends to the meeting, with the bold assertion that the Lord would heal them.

After the altar call, with nearly half of the audience responding, the evangelist announced he would pray for the deaf and the dumb. He asked that those who had brought persons with these afflictions to place fingers in their ears as he prayed for them. Argemiro prayed fervently for the deaf and dumb, first commanding all deaf and dumb spirits, "Leave, in the name of Jesus Christ!"

He prayed for any functional disorder of the ears themselves to be cleared up—being specific about nerves and blood vessels of the ear—the middle, inner and outer ear. Lastly, he shouted with a loud voice.

"Ephatha, be thou opened in Jesus name."

Then he said, "Now, friends, take your fingers out of the ears of the deaf and dumb. Let those who have been healed come forward!"

There was a stirring in the crowd. Soon dozens came to the platform, one after another. Within ten minutes, forty were standing in front of the crowd. One after another they came to the evangelist at the microphone. Tests were given to verify their deafness or dumbness and see whether they had been healed. Relatives testified to the facts before and after the event. It was obvious to all—God had worked miracles in healing a host of deaf and dumb people that night. Many of them had been deaf and dumb from their birth. It was the greatest demonstration of healing I had ever witnessed to that point of my Christian experience.

On our way back to the hotel from that meeting, Evangelist Froen spoke up.

"Mjorud, the same Holy Spirit that is working through Argemiro is in you and me. We have access to the same divine power! When I get to Jaffna, I am going to call the people to bring their deaf and dumb to our second meeting and believe the Lord for the *same thing!*"

I marveled at the faith of my co-worker.

Argemiro continued his crusade in Colombo with a reported twenty thousand attending his second meeting. There he specifically prayed for the blind and had similar success as with the deaf and dumb. His meetings pyramided to reach a reported sixty thousand attendance on the last day. His crusade shook the nation. People came from all over the island. There were so many miracles that reports of the meetings went in all directions causing a tremendous stir everywhere.

As planned, Froen went to the northernmost city, Jaffna, and during his first meeting announced, "Tomorrow evening I will pray for the deaf and dumb. Bring your loved ones and friends who are deaf or dumb to the meeting. The Lord will heal them!"

The attendance more than doubled the following evening. After the sermon, Froen asked those who had invited the deaf and dumb to bring them forward for prayer. Eighteen were brought forward. Froen expected just one or two to be healed in his first attempt thinking that if it failed, it would be of little consequence.

He placed his fingers in their ears and prayed as he had heard Argemiro pray. He prayed for each of the eighteen, and each of them was healed! The people in attendance were no less amazed than Froen. Attendance at his meetings mushroomed, too.

In the second of his meetings in the Anglican Church outside of Colombo, fourteen children from the deaf and dumb school were brought to the service. Froen prayed for all fourteen. All were healed. The next day Froen visited their school where the healing of all fourteen children was confirmed by electronic equipment.

I had gone to Nuwara Eliya as planned, but did not have the courage to step out in faith as Froen had done. From there I went to Kurunegala to hold meetings in an Anglican Church. The pastors were amazed at the large crowd, most of whom were Moslems.

A Moslem man, bedridden for years, had been miraculously healed at the Argemiro meetings. The former Moslem testified to his friends about his miracle. They concluded that the same thing would happen at *our* meetings. They brought hundreds of Moslems to our meeting that night, and one hundred ninety-nine Moslems accepted Christ and gave their names to our personal workers. Several miracles happened, too. An epileptic boy was completely delivered. A lame young woman was healed.

What happened in Sri Lanka while Argemiro, Froen and I were there started a chain reaction.

One of our friends and a national worker, Evangelist Jacob Perera, believed the same power released in our meetings could happen if *he* stepped out in faith and believed God. A month after we had left, Evangelist Perera started a crusade in a city north of Kandy.

"I believed God to work miracles through prayer," he reported. "It rained in our open air meetings every night, but the Lord worked miracles as I prayed the prayer of faith!"

Another national co-worker, Evangelist Verghese Chandy, president of Lanka Bible Institute, also began to believe the same way. He conducted three crusades and reported similar outstanding results.

Letters came from these men with wonderful news that the Lord was working through our dear friends in amazing ways. Here are quotes from letters written by Verghese Chandy in reporting on the first two meetings he conducted.

"Amazing things have happened! We have been thrust into a new dimension. In August we began by a period of fasting and prayer. God showed Hildy (Chandy's wife) where we were to hold a crusade in Jaffna. We went ahead ... and fifteen hundred came for the first night. I proclaimed the Gospel for some twenty-five minutes. Then, with fear and trembling, as we were directed in that vision, I prayed the mass prayer for the sick. A woman unable to walk for twenty-one years walked forward. A deaf and dumb woman was healed—and many others.

"The next day, three thousand came. Mighty miracles happened as we prayed the same way. The blind received their sight. A boy crippled for nineteen years came walking. The third day seven thousand came. And yesterday, twelve thousand; and so we extended the crusade, and Christopher Daniel will preach the next three days. Over five thousand have accepted Christ publicly thus far. I am moved to weeping when I think of Jesus' daily healing of the sick and moving among us so mightily.

"Daily the deaf and dumb are being healed. All manner of miracles have happened. Praise God! I just don't know where this ministry will lead us.

"Pray for God's guidance for us. We have forty workers who have come from many places to help us. There are meetings at seven-thirty and nine o'clock in the morning for the converts. Brother Ranjiit is conducting these teaching sessions. Over ninety percent of the people who are coming are Hindus. A mighty revival will come as a result of this crusade in Jaffna. It is amazing to all of us what faith in Jesus Christ can do. Please pray for all of us. This tremendous crusade is all so new to every one of us."

Several months later we received another letter from Evangelist Chandy concerning the second crusade he and his co-workers conducted in the city of Chilaw, on the western seaboard:

"The crusade just completed in Chilaw was glorious! This city is ten times smaller than Jaffna, but we had ten thousand out one night, with daily eight thousand to nine thousand hearing the Gospel. And all were witnesses to the miracles which Jesus did in their midst.... Thousands raised their hands to accept Christ.

"The miracles of healing far exceed that of Jaffna . . . . Crutches were thrown away and the lame walked in Jesus' name. Horrible leprosy on one girl's legs was all gone on the last evening! . . . It would take pages merely to list them all. We give all of the glory to Jesus!

"The impact and response was so great that Henry (one of last year's graduation class) is staying behind to start a revival center in Chilaw. He is renting the pavilion for meetings every Saturday."

19

ASTOUNDING HEALINGS

This correspondence stirred my own heart and faith. These men, with whom I had been associated for many years, were ordinary men with an ordinary ministry like my own. I prayed that when I arrived, knowing that I was indwelt with the same Holy Spirit, I would have a similar ministry.

Shortly thereafter, I was in Hawaii for a fourteen-day stint of preaching and meetings. One night at a meeting of young people, a young man came up to me with a prophecy. "You shall see power in healing and miracles like you have never seen before."

He was startled and did not understand his prophecy. I told him it was a confirmation from the Lord and that I was expecting God's power to be poured out when I arrived in Sri Lanka.

Christopher Daniel, a national missionary, shared the preaching with me at the first crusade. He, like Evangelist Chandy, had been used mightily by the Lord in open air crusades in other cities. He was well acquainted with the procedure of the mass prayer that had brought about so many miracles in previous meetings.

"I want you to pray for the sick after the sermon tonight," I informed Daniel. "I want to see *how* you pray. Later in the week, you preach and I'll pray for the sick."

"That is fine with me," he answered. "It is a matter of faith. Believing God to work miracles according to His Word brings such power in prayer. Brother Chandy was being used in this powerful new way. After a few meetings, he asked that I step out and believe God to do the same things through me. I did and was astounded to see what God could do, even through me."

Then I thought: *Daniel studied the methods of prayer power of Chandy. Now I am his understudy, believing the Lord can use even me—as he is using these two men of faith.*

The first evening, two thousand people gathered at the crusade site, a combination football stadium and fairgrounds. I preached the gospel message, and three hundred to four hundred people raised hands to make decisions for Jesus Christ. Following the personal work, Daniel took charge of the meeting for the healing service.

"Jesus Christ will not heal you if you are trusting in some other god, idol or charm," he said. "Those of you who have charms take them off and hand them to the ushers."

Ushers went through the crowd with baskets and collected the charms. They were placed in a pile on the raised platform. Then Daniel began his prayer.

"In the name of Jesus," he proclaimed, "I deny the powers of demons and curses, deny the powers of sickness and disease. In Christ I break the power of the charms, and claim freedom and liberty for those gathered here to be healed by Jesus Christ!"

Then he prayed fervently and specifically for the blind, deaf and dumb, lame, and for those afflicted with pains, disease and sicknesses. It was a long prayer.

When he concluded his prayer, he said, "Those who have been healed, come forward, make contact with one of the ushers, and come and testify."

The ushers verified the claims to keep order. Those with spurious claims or looking only for attention would be quietly led aside.

At one point an usher led an elderly man up on the platform. Daniel spoke to him.

"What did Jesus do for you?"

"Jesus healed my eyes. I was blind."

"How long were you blind?"

"I have been totally blind for five years."

Many in the audience knew him, knew of his blindness. They began clapping their hands with happiness.

"How many fingers am I holding up?" asked Daniel.

"Three," the man replied correctly.

By the time the first man had testified, a number of others were led to the platform. The next to testify was a young man formerly unable to speak. His dumbness was the result of a birth defect, and he had never been able to utter any sound. Daniel verified that he was no longer dumb. He could now imitate sounds and was joyful at hearing the strange sound of his own voice.

Two testified who had been partially paralyzed. Both were healed and able to move their formerly limp limbs. It was obvious that the Lord was there to work miracles.

The next night our crowd had increased to thirty-five hundred. We followed the same format as the night before. I preached and Daniel conducted the healing service—with more miracles.

There were more than four thousand the third evening. I had all I could do to keep from weeping to see their response to the Gospel. More than two thousand stood to their feet to receive Christ. They recited the sinners' prayer and indicated their acceptance of Jesus Christ as Savior and Lord by raising their hands.

This continued throughout the crusade—night after night. However, I felt I had to try the mass prayer and pray even as did my co-worker Daniel.

In a morning convert class of seven hundred, before praying for the sick, I asked, "How many here are suffering from a bad heart? Raise your hands." I had great faith in this respect because the Lord had used me so many previous times to heal people afflicted with heart trouble. About fifteen hands were raised.

"Put one hand over your heart as I pray for you," I said. They all responded. Then I prayed for them, believing the Lord would touch and heal them. I then asked, "If you *know* that the Lord has healed your heart because you felt healing fire flow into your body, stand up." I was amazed. All of them stood!

I prayed for those who had been brought there who were deaf and dumb. A twenty-two-year-old youth testified he had been healed.

Then I prayed for the lame. While I was still praying, a woman stood up, shouting praises to God for her healing. I received my confidence!

Our next crusade was in Batticoloa. Doubts assailed me as I prayed. My prayer was hurried and, I knew, lacked confidence. I wondered whether I had bobbled a great opportunity. After prayer, I asked those who had been healed to come forward. No one responded. My faith began to waver. Finally, a young woman came forward. She testified in a calm, easy way, "I have been healed of a headache."

Oh, no, I thought to myself. *Anybody can get rid of a headache—what does this prove?*

"My headache has lasted six months," the young woman continued. "I have been to many doctors. None has helped. And no medication I tried took away the pain. But as you prayed tonight, it was as though a breath came from heaven and swept all over my body. I have been completely healed of my headache!"

Another came to testify—an elderly man. He said his vision had been so "fogged" for four years that he could not distinguish people he knew very well. Happily, he told how the Lord had touched him; had removed the "fog" from his eyes. Now he could see clearly!

These large meetings with astounding healings had their place in the outreach for the Kingdom. The entire nation was talking about the miracles of God after the Argemiro meetings and the large open air meetings conducted by us. They confronted a whole island nation with the reality of a living God and the authority which a Christian possesses to believe Him to perform what He has promised in the Bible.

But we soon learned that most people came because of curiosity. They wanted to see and hear about the healing miracles.

They came to be healed themselves, and in their desire for healing, many made superficial decisions for Christ—thinking this would enhance their chances of being healed. The permanent results after these crusades were disappointing. While several thousand might raise their hands for salvation and pray to receive Christ, actual additions in evangelical churches proved minimal.

About seven hundred sincere believers from the meetings turned out for follow-up meetings a week after the Badulla crusade. These meetings were held every weekend, but the attendance diminished until less than a hundred came.

I studied the matter and learned this was the story generally for all the crusades. Many factors accounted for this poor showing. First, we didn't have trained pastors and workers to begin churches for the new converts. Second, many who responded lived far from the community, and bus travel to church services was too expensive for them. Third, ostracism for embracing a new religion took its toll. The state religion is Buddhism, and the fear of losing one's job deterred some new Christians from associating with other believers.

We decided on a long-range program to build local congregations. Our great need was trained pastors. The Bible school we began trained men for the ministry, but graduates with two years of elementary Bible training were not really prepared. They needed further study in a seminary. But this was not available, so they had to get their experience from internship for several years under a proven pastor.

The following year a cholera epidemic prevented us from having the large open air meetings. This proved providential, however, because we were able to meet with local congregations. It worked! Now there are many new congregations coming into being with believers who come for worship and the hearing of God's Word. Our primary concern is still the lack of trained workers to accomplish the task. So another Bible school has now been started by nationals to train workers.

Meanwhile, the Lord also has demonstrated His power to perform miracles in many other countries as well. Lack of faith blocked significant healings in Germany. But not in Norway.

In eight different cities miracles happened in every place during the mass prayer for healing! The healing miracles were not as extensive as in Sri Lanka but the meetings were in churches, with smaller crowds.

The mass prayer for healing brings about the most astounding results in large gatherings. I discovered this as I began traveling again in the United States.

The Word of God states that "the prayer of faith will heal the sick." I experienced the truth of this verse in Sri Lanka. God's Word is true, whether one person is praying for another or whether the mass prayer is prayed at a large gathering. The Lord works everywhere people assert their authority to pray with faith in His Word and under the anointing of His Spirit.

Not all for whom I prayed have been healed. There are some Christians in wheel chairs who have been prayed for by many evangelists. They have been anointed with oil. Yet their sickness remains. Why? I don't know.

Yes, I was soon to learn the testing of faith in this matter firsthand, and experience a spiritual crisis as never before in my life.

20

THE BATTLE IS TO KEEP
OUR EYES ON THE LORD

While writing the manuscript for this book a year ago, in January, I was under discomfort while sitting. Not knowing the cause, I asked a doctor, and he gave the opinion that I had deep-seated varicose veins. Believing this to be the cause of my affliction, I persisted at my writing. But the discomfort grew worse from long hours at my typewriter.

In February, on another world evangelistic tour, I had the same discomfort. But this time I also had a swelling on my left gonad (testicle). I wondered if there was a single cause for both.

However, I wasn't concerned. I believed the Lord would intervene while enroute and deliver me from my distress.

While in East Java for a large crusade, I decided to fast and pray for my sickness, as I had done to heal myself in the past. I fasted eight days, but my prayer time was primarily concerned about the meetings. The theater we rented was packed out. Thousands were turned away each night. Hundreds were converted to Jesus and healed. On the third night I asked how many of the audience had been healed during the first two nights of the meetings. Several hundred stood.

I recall saying to the Lord, "With all of these healed, why not me, Lord?"

I still had great discomfort but was full of energy. There was no slackening in pace because of my ailment, whatever it was. However, three weeks later, as I preached in an open air crusade in northern Sri Lanka, I was stricken with an excruciating pain. I called for the Reverend Christopher Daniel, who was seated on the platform, to come and pray for me. He laid hands upon me, prayed, and claimed healing for me while I continued to preach.

The pain subsided somewhat and I was able to conclude the sermon and the healing service which followed. I felt a bit better the next day, but there was no change to detect. Several co-workers came by to pray for my healing.

I pondered my predicament and wondered why the Lord was delaying His answer.

Two days later I came to Colombo. We traveled six hours at a time by car. The pain was at times almost unbearable. I decided to see a doctor and find out the exact cause of my sickness so I could pray more specifically.

I called Dr. Vere Ederesinghe whom I had met in a crusade two years before. He had come to a meeting—an avowed atheist with a drinking problem—and had received Christ as His Savior and deliverance from alcoholism.

Within an hour Dr. Ederesinghe was in my room.

"Have you ever had serious pains in your legs?"

"Yes. When I came to Norway last spring I had what I thought was arthritis in both knees. It almost crippled me," I answered. "But I claimed healing and within a week it was gone."

"You were going from warm to colder climates when you experienced that release from those symptoms?"

"Why, yes. We kept going north in Norway until we met raw, cold weather with snow."

"How about other pains or symptoms in the last two or three years?"

"I've had this discomfort when sitting for over three years. I've also had some serious attacks of vertigo in the past two years. Sometimes I'd even fall right to the floor," I informed him.

"You have been in many places here in Sri Lanka preaching the Gospel in the past years?"

"Yes, I've spent about one month every year traveling here

for the past six years," I answered.

"You have *filariasis!*" the doctor said decisively.

"Filariasis? I have never heard of it. What kind of a sickness is that?"

"Filariasis comes from a mosquito bite like malaria," he explained. "One bite from a mosquito carries an infinitesimally small larva—filariae—of the parasite into your blood stream. From that larva, millions of small hairlike parasites develop. They make their home in your lymphatic system and feed upon your blood! They move through your blood system while you are sleeping. Your attack of vertigo was their seige in your inner ear. That attack upon your knees which you likened to arthritis is also characteristic of their behavior. They work in the manner of beavers. They build 'dams' in the body, closing off a section as they intended to do in your legs. They multiply exceedingly and control the flow of the blood into that area to keep themselves alive. When they multiply in a leg closed off at the knee, the result is called *Elephantiasis.* While you were traveling north in Norway and coming into a colder climate, the parasites went into hibernation which is typical of their behavior."

I was amazed at his knowledge of this disease that I'd never heard of. I asked him about it.

"Would you believe, Evangelist Mjorud, that I am a world reknown filariasis specialist?" The doctor smiled. "I took *your* 'prescription' when I came forward two years ago. Now you are going to take mine."

He wrote on a prescription pad and sent a couple of national workers out to fetch the medicine.

"You are a clinical case," he said. "You will need rest for several weeks as you take this medicine."

"I'll try to be as good a patient for you as you were for me," I answered.

"The cure will be over a period of many days," the doctor said. "The parasites cannot be killed all at once. Your blood would be overloaded in housekeeping duties from the many dead carcasses. You must take this medicine for twenty-one days, then stop for three months. Then you will take the *hetrazan* medicine for only another four days and stop for another three months. That is the cycle—four days with medicine, three months without. These parasites are nearly impossible to kill off entirely."

There were four bottles of different pills. Dr. Ederesinghe stayed until I had taken his prescription.

"Tomorrow you'll wish that you had never called me. You will feel nauseated, listless and out of sorts. Just stay in bed and rest," he said.

"But I am preaching tomorrow noon and tomorrow evening," I protested.

"No, you will do no preaching tomorrow," he insisted. "You won't be up to it at all. Get substitutes to take your place."

The doctor left and I knelt to pray with my co-worker and traveling campanion, John Kittleson. I claimed the promise of Mark 16:18: "If they drink any deadly thing, it will not hurt them." We asked the Lord to give me strength and vitality to meet all my commitments, not only the next day, but for the rest of the trip.

As the result of our prayers, the pills had just the opposite effect on me as what the doctor said. Instead of feeling nauseated and listless, I had such vitality and vigor that I amazed everyone who knew about my sickness. I preached vigorously at both noon and evening services the following day. Even the doctor was amazed.

"This has to be the power of the Lord!" he exclaimed.

Three days later, I went to Bombay, India, for a seven-day crusade. My health and vigor prevailed even though I continued with the medications. The pain was gone, the swelling subsided, and I was sure the twenty-one day treatment would end my problem. I continued on to West Germany and Norway. Shortly after coming to Norway, twenty-one days had expired so I stopped taking medication.

But one night, two months later, I had an attack. It struck the small of my back. The next night pain hit me near the shoulder. I was suffering another invasion of the parasites! I went right back on the *hetrazan,* as the doctor had advised, for another twenty-one-day stretch. Within a few days the pain and swelling on my back was gone. I felt fine again and continued my schedule of teaching and preaching.

But within two months, I was attacked again. I had used a medical doctor only for physical examinations and vaccine shots in the past. The clinic where I went for these had several doctors, but none of them knew a thing about filariasis. A druggist from whom I had purchased the *hetrazan* pointed out a general form that came with the drug. From this I saw I was taking only a half dosage. The drug is prescribed according to weight. The doctor had prescribed the medication for one with the weight of a typical Ceylonese!

I met with Dr. J. B. Friberg, who had been a medical missionary in Africa, to see if he had any knowledge of filariasis.

"Yes," he replied. "I ran into it in Africa!"

I told him my whole story. He recommended I increase the dosage of the *hetrazan* according to that described in the drug circular. He also asked that I submit to a thorough physical examination, which he gave me.

I went on my third twenty-one-day series of this medication, this time at twice the dosage. I learned from the circular that this drug is harmless to the body, so I continued on after the twenty-one days were up, for forty-four days in all. I had no further signs of filariae activity except for discomfort in sitting and the swollen gonad. I had a busy summer schedule with Bible camps and conferences, but gave in to Dr. Friberg's request to see him.

I visited his office September 1, and returned two days later for the results of my physical. "Computerized" blood tests were negative—and so were all the other tests. Then the doctor examined the swollen gonad.

"Mjorud, that testicle has to be removed. From the symptoms, I advise immediate surgery."

He called in a pathologist. After a thorough questioning, he advised the same thing. I was shaken. Both physicians advised immediate surgery and urged me to go at once to the hospital. I wanted to delay and pray. But these two Christian medical men indicated an obvious concern for my welfare.

"I will phone my wife, then give you my answer," I said.
I went to a phone booth and prayed earnestly. The Lord said clearly, "Be not afraid. Go ahead with the surgery." This was a complete surprise to me.

Then I phoned Gundhild and gave her all the details—including the Lord's directive. She agreed that I should follow the Lord's guidance. I went immediately to Dr. Friberg's office and gave him my consent for the surgery.

The next day I was in the hospital, my first such experience in my life. I was slated for surgery the following morning. I committed myself, the doctors, and surgery to the Lord and rested very peacefully. The surgery itself was rather uneventful. The gonad was removed.

The afternoon after surgery my doctor came with the lab report on the removed gonad. "You had *terato carcinoma* (cancer) with *four types of maligant tissue!* But as far as we could observe, everything has been removed and the surgery was a success."

What a shock. After my visit with Dr. Ederesinghe, I had blamed filariae parasites for that swollen gonad. But instead of having one deadly disease attacking my body, I had *two!*

On the second day after surgery, the head diagnostician came with this report: "I recommend further surgery for you. This will be rather radical, to remove the lining of your scrotum and several hundred lymph nodes in the abdominal cavity. This surgery is both preventive and diagnostic."

Lord, will it never end? was my inner thought. I replied, "I'll have to give that serious thought and prayer before giving you my answer."

Later Dr. Friberg came to visit. I told him the bad news I had received.

"Take it easy, Mjorud," the doctor counseled. "You have the Lord with you, and most medical men are just human—statisticians. We know your chances of longevity are better with further surgery, that's all. But we doctors don't always take into account the spiritual equation. You put this matter before the Lord. Get your answer from Him."

I went home three days after my hospital stay. I followed the advice of my doctor and prayed until I received an answer. It was, *"No further surgery!"* On my next visit to Dr. Friberg's office I told him the word that I had from the Lord.

"Well, praise the Lord! That's my answer for you, too!" he said.

"Praise the Lord!" I echoed, relieved that he wasn't an ally to the recommendation for radical surgery.

My convalescence was slow and painful, but nothing compared to the onslaught on my mind. I felt like Job after Satan had brought disasters down on him. Job had "friends" who came to "console" him. But they gave him nothing but philosophical arguments that his afflictions came as punishment from God. They tried to convince him that his sins and derelictions in the faith caused his problems.

I remembered that the Scriptures plainly reveal that Job's difficulties were not from God, but from Satan. Job was a righteous man before God.

It seemed I had more than three "friends" to assail my mind. I battled the philosophical thoughts that Job struggled with. Warfare in the mind is very subtle and difficult to understand. I have never feared introspection and I was driven by my thoughts in this direction. I wondered if there was some lack of obedience, some hidden fault, or some waywardness on my part, that had caused God to take away the "hedge," permitting Satan to assail me. I was convinced that Satan had laid both sicknesses upon me. The "hedge" was not taken away from Job because of any wrongdoing. Rather, it was just an understanding of the fact that God, in His permissive will, often permits the "righteous" to be stricken along with the ungodly. Just as with Job, we cry out to God, asking, "Why me, Lord?" And often the answer is silence. I studied the case of Job quite carefully, lest I blame God instead of Satan.

The will of God sometimes is inscrutable even to Christians. So it was with me. There were so many imponderable "whys."

Why were my prayers ineffective for myself while effective for others?

Why was I not healed by the prayers of my co-workers when they were instruments for healing others?

How could I claim healing for other cancer victims when failing to receive that same healing for myself?

With every twinge of pain, thoughts clouded with doubt taunted me: *Maybe the doctors are right. Perhaps cancer is even now attacking and spreading throughout my lymph glands!*

It was not easy to ward off negative thoughts. For several days I wrestled with the thought, *I'd better keep this surgery from the public. If the news gets out, it will ruin my ministry.*

But I met that head-on and resolved that that thought was of the devil. I vowed to tell the truth. God doesn't have to defend His ways to us.

How difficult to "fight the good fight of faith" when your body is racked with pain and with thoughts of two possibly deadly diseases, filariasis and cancer. Gundhild and I systematically confessed our faith, and the healing virtue of Christ in prayer and worship. The Spirit of God brought inner peace and joy. The battle was to keep our eyes upon the Lord and His Word, for these are the spiritual weapons to tear down enemy strongholds in our mind. The Lord never promised eternal blue skies. But He is with us through storms, testings and trials.

With his eye upon the Lord, Peter walked upon the surging waves. Likewise, we can walk calmly above our circumstances when we keep our eyes upon the Lord.

Friends phoned from all over the United States. They assured me of their prayers. Letters of encouragement came by the scores, all telling me prayer groups were praying for me.

Two weeks later my friend, Dr. Friberg, came with another sober report.

"A clinical study by a number of cancer specialists advise the same surgery recommended by the head diagnostician," he said. I wondered if he had changed his mind and if this was his recommendation, too. I didn't dare ask him.

Further assaults came to my mind. *Mjorud, you've lost faith. Better have that radical surgery before it's too late.*

Once again I went to the Lord on the matter. After much struggle and prayer, the same answer came back: "No further surgery."

Something wonderful happened to both my wife and me. We continued in long seasons of prayer and praise together, morning and evening, wherein we positively claimed scriptural promises for healing. We wove these promises together into a spontaneous confession of faith in what the Bible said. Peace and joy began to well up within our hearts and minds. As I persevered in this practice day after day, there came a positive conviction that the Lord had undertaken—all symptoms, advice and reasonings to the contrary notwithstanding.

We had won a victory through the Word of God in our minds, which I now count as one of my greatest.

I visited Dr. Friberg a few days later. "Well, Herb, what have you decided to do regarding the clinical advisory?" he asked.

"The Lord has given me the same answer as before—'No further surgery,' " I said.

"That's the answer the Lord has given me, too. I have really prayed much about this, Herb. I believe you are in the Lord's hands."

Then came the good news. Hospital X-rays of my lymphatic system and lab reports revealed no traces of cancer. I also had another blood test for filariasis and that proved negative, too.

About a week later, I received separate letters from two co-workers in Sri Lanka that were a source of great inspiration.

One reads:

"From the time I received your letter, my wife, two children, and all at the center have been praying for you daily. But there was no clear message from the Lord. Then on the third inst. at two-thirty a.m. the Lord awoke me and directed me to pray for you. In the course of the prayer, the Lord said that *He has healed you,* dear brother! And to confirm this, Bertram Casinader (a dear brother and co-worker in Trincomalee) wrote me yesterday that on the first inst. one of his friends who attends Bertram's meetings while praying was told by the Lord that you would be healed in three days. The Lord loves you very dearly, dear brother, and that is why there is such a host of people who have been commissioned to pray for you. I believe that when this reaches you, the doctors would have reported that you have been miraculously healed. Praise be His glorious name, Jehovah-Rapha *(I am the Lord, thy Healer).* "

I looked at the chronology of events. My blood test was on the sixth, revealing no filariasis. The X-ray tests on the tenth revealed no cancer! The Lord revealed to two different people, half way around the world, that I was healed totally of both diseases *three days before my examinations!*

Perhaps I'll never completely know *why* the Lord permits testings such as these. However, I now know, partially, something the sick go through when they are afflicted. I am now better equipped "to comfort them with the comfort where of I was comforted." Trials are difficult, but the Word does say, *"Count all trials for joy,* for trials work patience, steadfastness, approvedness, and hope that does not put to shame." I learned lessons in faith and obedience that I could never have learned except through having these experiences.

This truth, plus the assurance of our authority to believe in all that God promises in His Word, the Bible, provides both you and me all that we need for a completely satisfying, joyous and exciting life—both here and hereafter.

The Wonderful Way of Living

Christian Life

One of the most talked about in-spirational magazines today . . . Colorful personality profiles . . . skilled analyses of world trends in light of the Bible . . . Poignant narratives . . . wide ranging reports on the latest in helpful books and records.

Membership in Christian Life brings you this exciting monthly magazine plus Ten Additional Bonus Features including discounts on the best in books and records.

ORDER NOW AND SAVE

☐Yes, please enter a membership in Christian Life for twelve months for $9 (for foreign subscriptions add $3 per year for postage).

Name_____

Address_____

City_____State_____Zip____

☐ Enter or extend a two year membership at $16 (you save $2).

☐ Enter or extend a membership for three years at $21 (you save $6).

Remarkable Accounts of Spiritual Revival World-Wide

from  Creation House

Like a Mighty Wind, *by Mel Tari*
An eye-witness account of the astonishing Indonesian revival. Thousands converted to Christ, the dead raised to life, water turned to wine. Paper $1.75

Look Out! The Pentecostals Are Coming, *by Peter Wagner*
Throughout Latin America a massive revival is under way. Dr. Wagner of Fuller Seminary explains how and why. Cloth $4.95

Fire in the Philippines, *by Jim Montgomery*
A remarkable study of the elements of spiritual revival which today is engulfing whole communities in this island archipelago. Cloth $4.95

For This Cross I'll Kill You, *by Bruce Olson*
One man with vision and faith sees a whole tribe discover Jesus Christ in the jungles of Colombia, reorganize its tribal customs and then share its faith with enemy tribes. Cloth $4.95

The Holy Spirit in Vietnam, *by Orrel Steinkamp*
The story nobody knows—miracles of conversion to Christ, physical healings, the dead raised to life in a war-torn country. Cloth $4.95